GRAPHIC SCIENCE BIOGRAPHIES

CHARLES DARWIN AND THE THEORY OF EVOLUTION

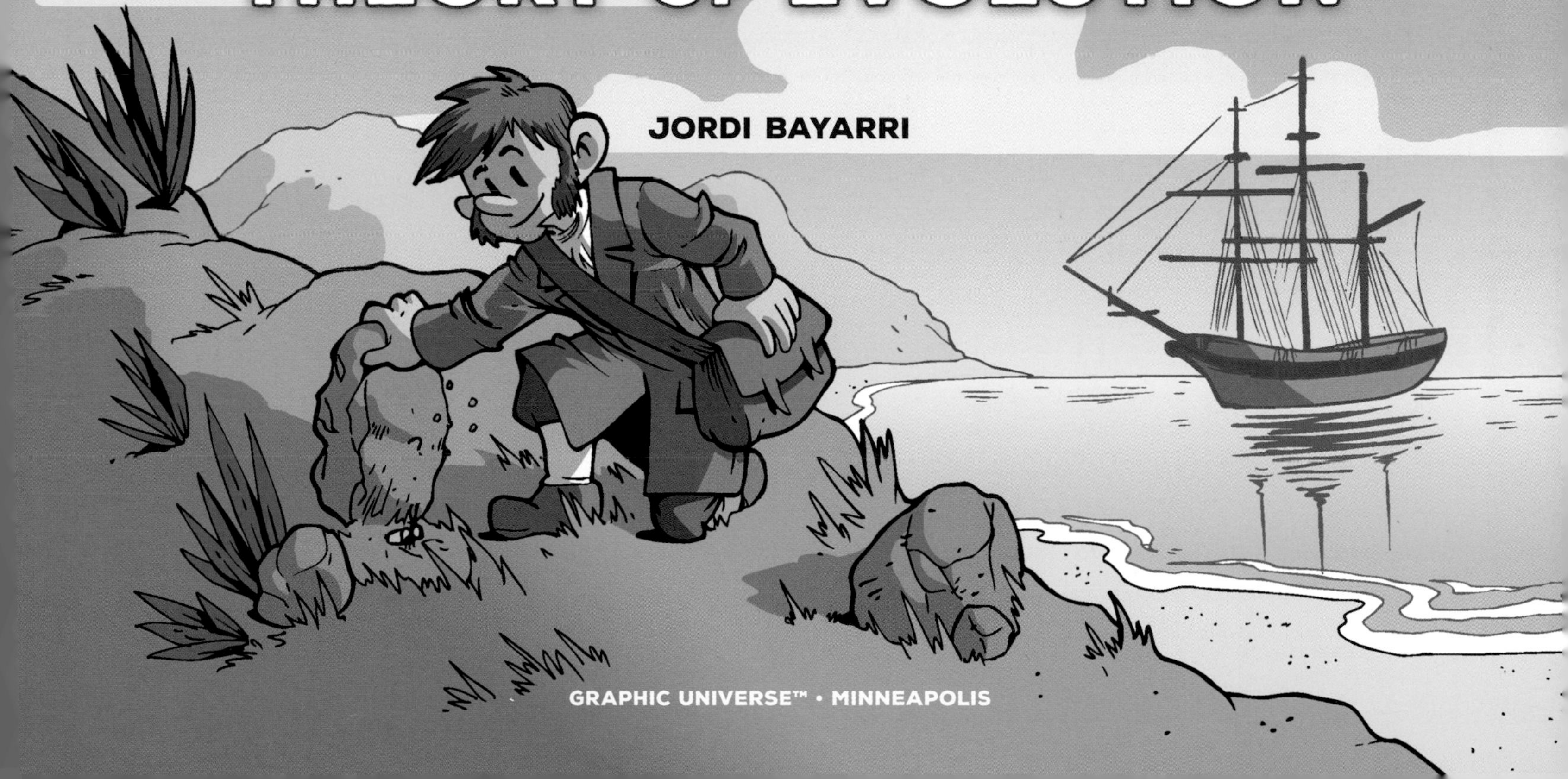

JORDI BAYARRI

GRAPHIC UNIVERSE™ • MINNEAPOLIS

Story and art by Jordi Bayarri
Coloring by Dani Seijas
Historical and scientific consultation by Dr. Tayra M. C. Lanuza-Navarro, PhD in History of Science
Translation by Dr. Tayra M. C. Lanuza-Navarro and Carin Berkowitz

First American edition published in 2020 by Graphic Universe™

Graphic Universe™
An imprint of Lerner Publishing Group, Inc.
241 First Avenue North
Minneapolis, MN 55401 USA

For reading levels and more information, look up this title at www.lernerbooks.com.

Image credit: Wellcome Library, p. 37

Main body text set in CCDaveGibbonsLower.
Typeface provided by OpenType.

Library of Congress Cataloging-in-Publication Data

Names: Bayarri, Jordi, 1972- author, illustrator.
Title: Charles Darwin and the theory of evolution / Jordi Bayarri.
Description: Minneapolis : Graphic Universe, [2020] I Series: Graphic science biographies I Audience: Age 10–14. I Audience: Grade 7 to 8. I Includes bibliographical references and index.
Identifiers: LCCN 2019006972 I ISBN 9781541578227 (lb : alk. paper)
Subjects: LCSH: Darwin, Charles, 1809–1882. I Naturalists—England—Biography—Juvenile literature. I Evolution (Biology)—Juvenile literature.
Classification: LCC QH31.D2 B395 2020 I DDC 576.8/2092 [B]—dc23

LC record available at https://lccn.loc.gov/2019006972

Manufactured in the United States of America
1-46927-47807-5/20/2019

CONTENTS

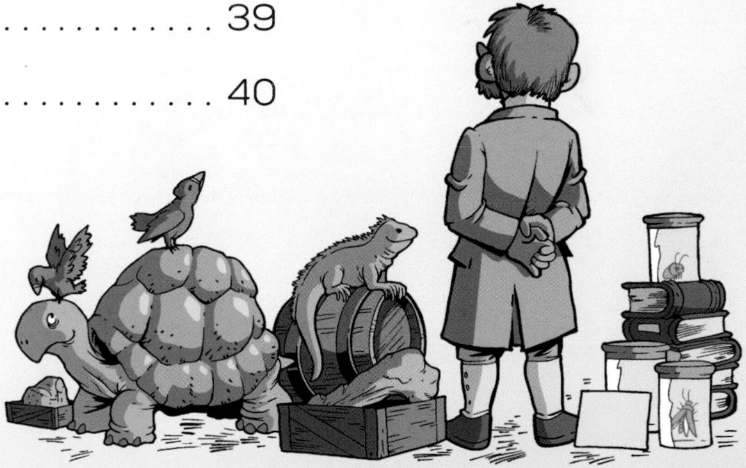

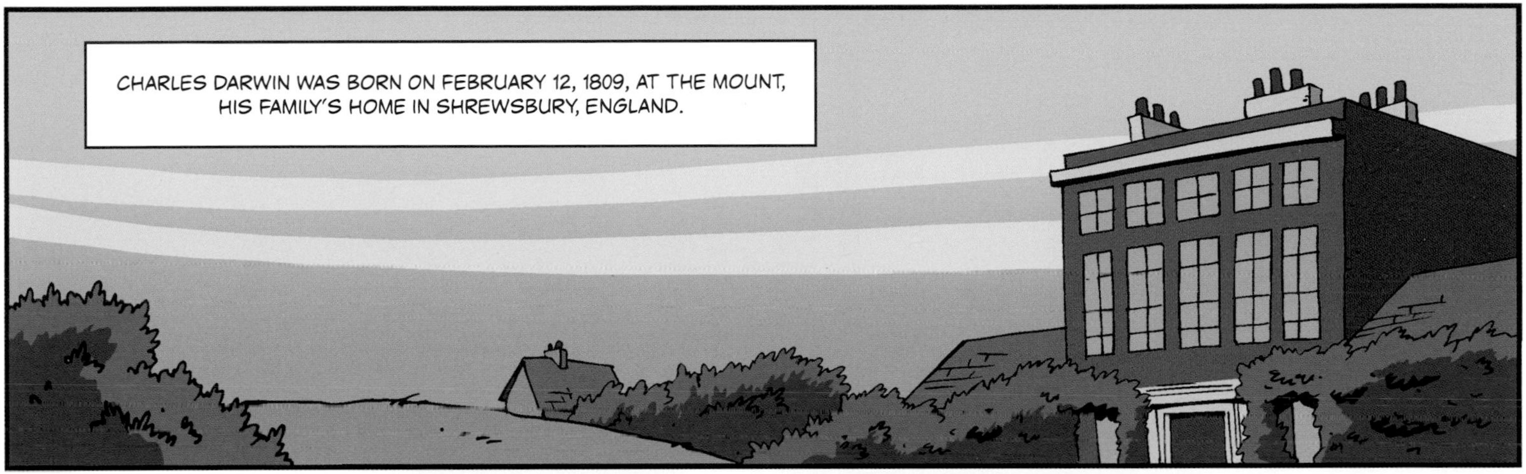
CHARLES DARWIN WAS BORN ON FEBRUARY 12, 1809, AT THE MOUNT, HIS FAMILY'S HOME IN SHREWSBURY, ENGLAND.

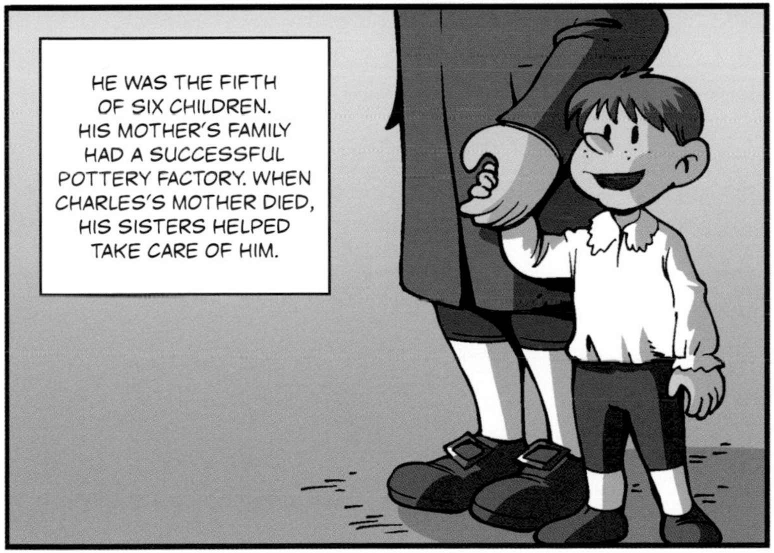
HE WAS THE FIFTH OF SIX CHILDREN. HIS MOTHER'S FAMILY HAD A SUCCESSFUL POTTERY FACTORY. WHEN CHARLES'S MOTHER DIED, HIS SISTERS HELPED TAKE CARE OF HIM.

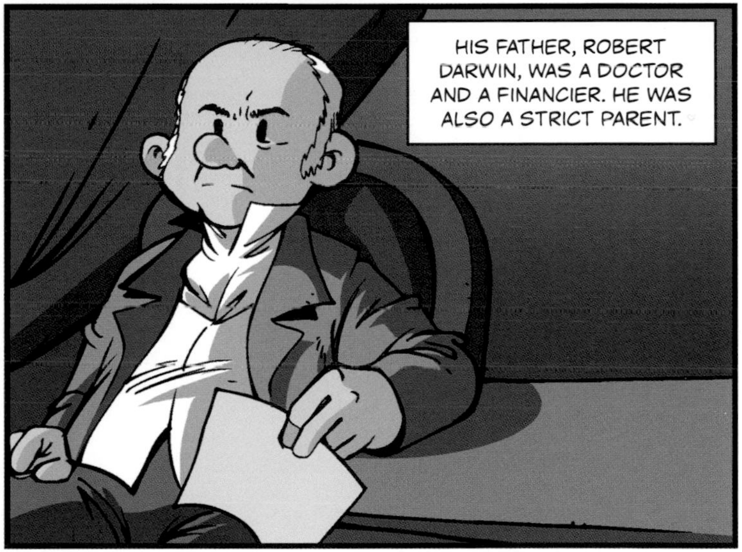
HIS FATHER, ROBERT DARWIN, WAS A DOCTOR AND A FINANCIER. HE WAS ALSO A STRICT PARENT.

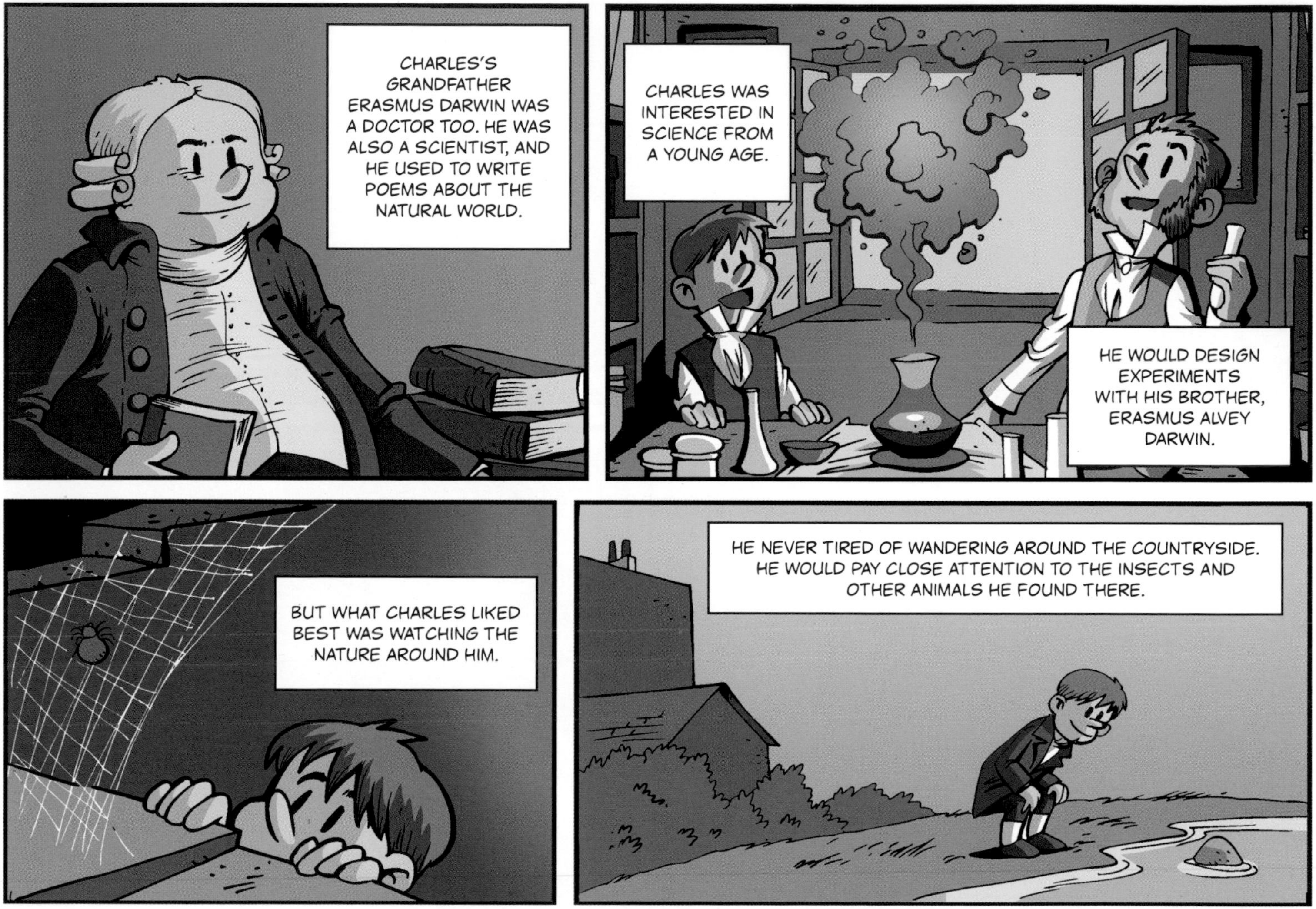
CHARLES'S GRANDFATHER ERASMUS DARWIN WAS A DOCTOR TOO. HE WAS ALSO A SCIENTIST, AND HE USED TO WRITE POEMS ABOUT THE NATURAL WORLD.
CHARLES WAS INTERESTED IN SCIENCE FROM A YOUNG AGE.
HE WOULD DESIGN EXPERIMENTS WITH HIS BROTHER, ERASMUS ALVEY DARWIN.
BUT WHAT CHARLES LIKED BEST WAS WATCHING THE NATURE AROUND HIM.
HE NEVER TIRED OF WANDERING AROUND THE COUNTRYSIDE. HE WOULD PAY CLOSE ATTENTION TO THE INSECTS AND OTHER ANIMALS HE FOUND THERE.

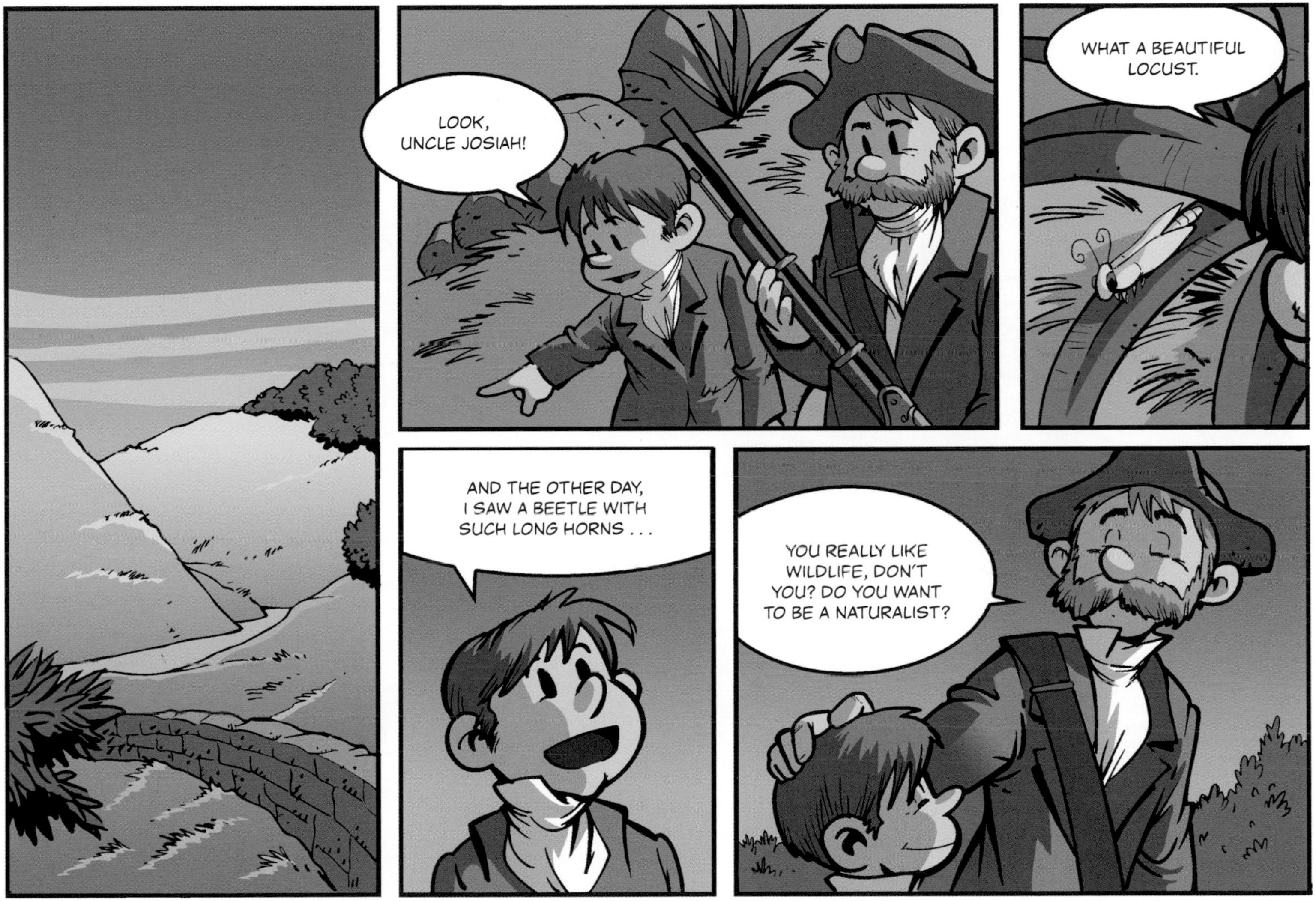
LOOK, UNCLE JOSIAH!
WHAT A BEAUTIFUL LOCUST.
AND THE OTHER DAY, I SAW A BEETLE WITH SUCH LONG HORNS . . .
YOU REALLY LIKE WILDLIFE, DON'T YOU? DO YOU WANT TO BE A NATURALIST?

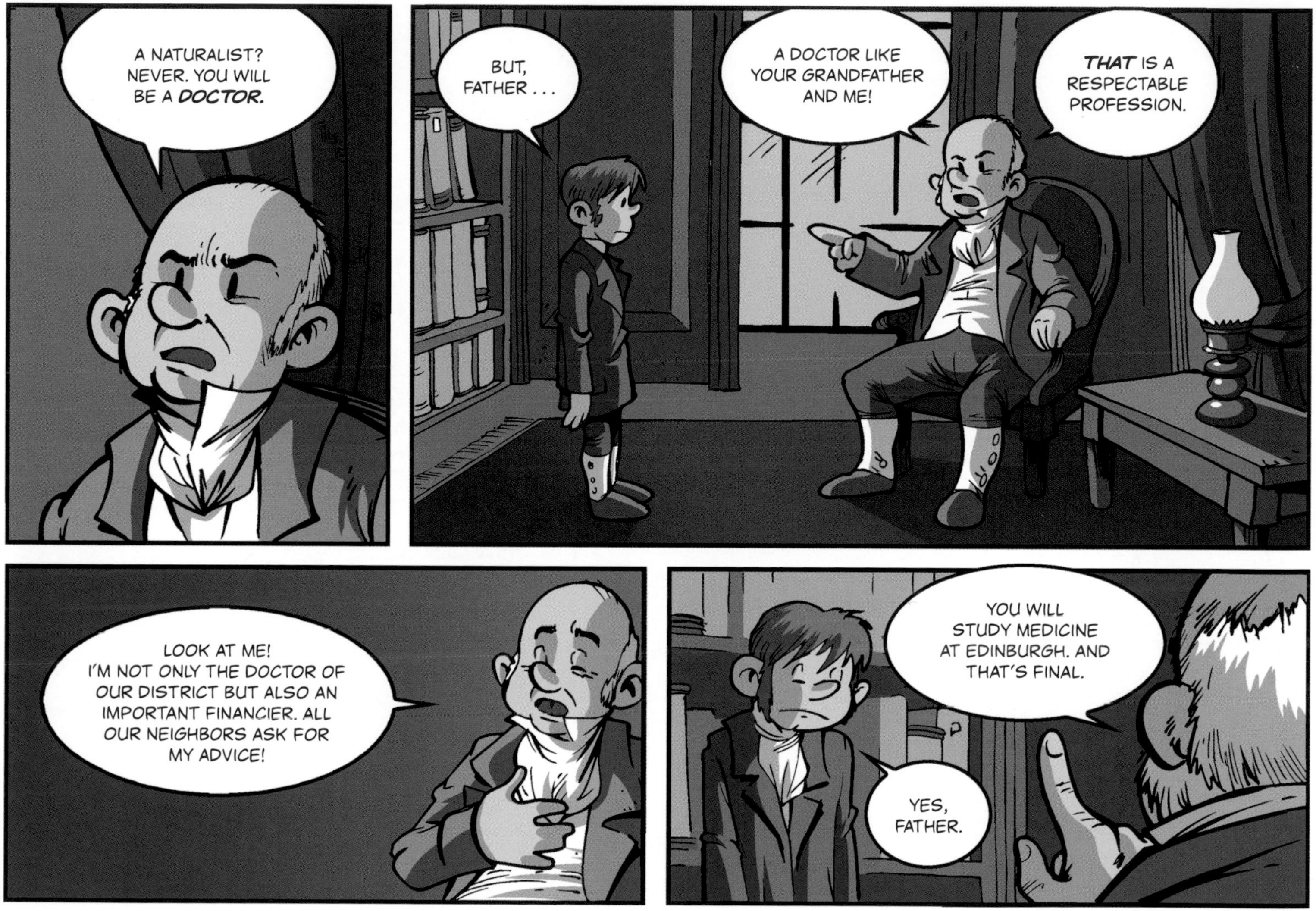
A NATURALIST? NEVER. YOU WILL BE A ***DOCTOR.***
BUT, FATHER . . .
A DOCTOR LIKE YOUR GRANDFATHER AND ME!
THAT IS A RESPECTABLE PROFESSION.
LOOK AT ME! I'M NOT ONLY THE DOCTOR OF OUR DISTRICT BUT ALSO AN IMPORTANT FINANCIER. ALL OUR NEIGHBORS ASK FOR MY ADVICE!
YOU WILL STUDY MEDICINE AT EDINBURGH. AND THAT'S FINAL.
YES, FATHER.

EDINBURGH, SCOTLAND, 1825

WELCOME TO OUR NEXT ANATOMY LESSON.

TODAY WE'LL DISSECT THIS BODY AND EXAMINE ITS INTESTINES.

GULP!

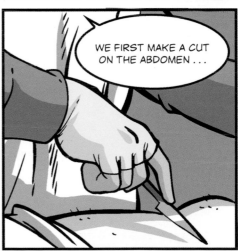

WE FIRST MAKE A CUT ON THE ABDOMEN . . .

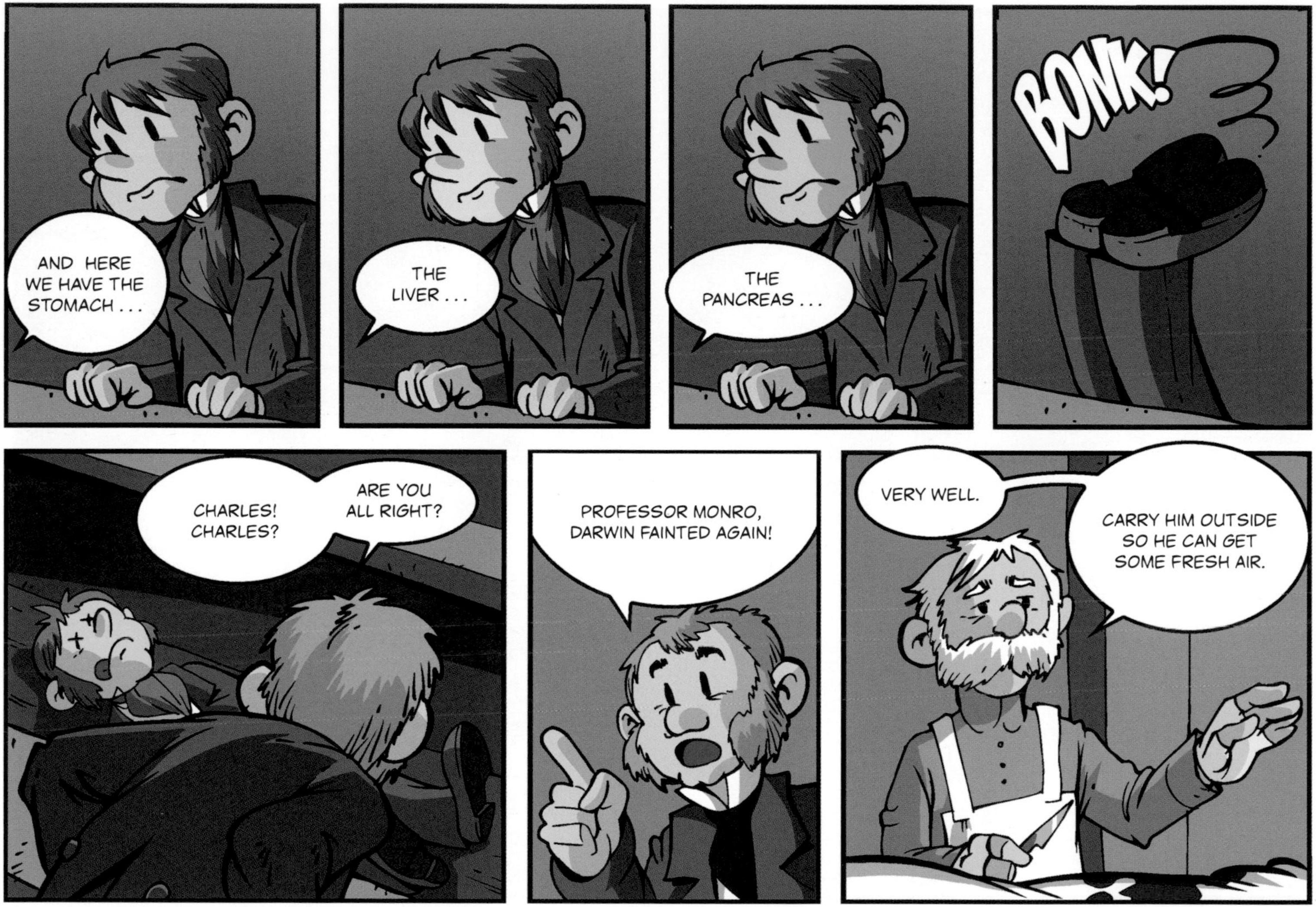
AND HERE WE HAVE THE STOMACH . . .
THE LIVER . . .
THE PANCREAS . . .
BONK!
CHARLES! CHARLES?
ARE YOU ALL RIGHT?
PROFESSOR MONRO, DARWIN FAINTED AGAIN!
VERY WELL.
CARRY HIM OUTSIDE SO HE CAN GET SOME FRESH AIR.

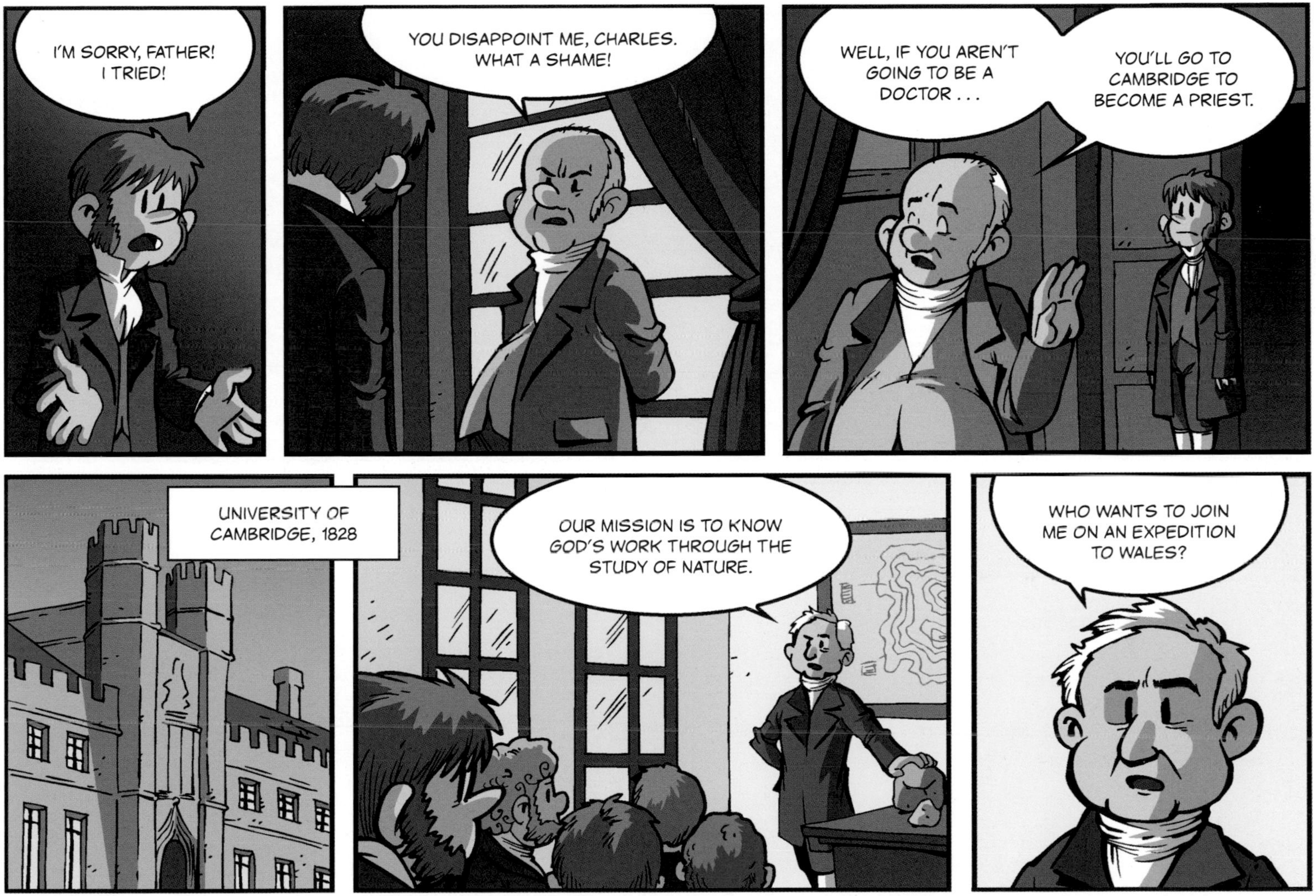
I'M SORRY, FATHER! I TRIED!
YOU DISAPPOINT ME, CHARLES. WHAT A SHAME!
WELL, IF YOU AREN'T GOING TO BE A DOCTOR . . .
YOU'LL GO TO CAMBRIDGE TO BECOME A PRIEST.
UNIVERSITY OF CAMBRIDGE, 1828
OUR MISSION IS TO KNOW GOD'S WORK THROUGH THE STUDY OF NATURE.
WHO WANTS TO JOIN ME ON AN EXPEDITION TO WALES?

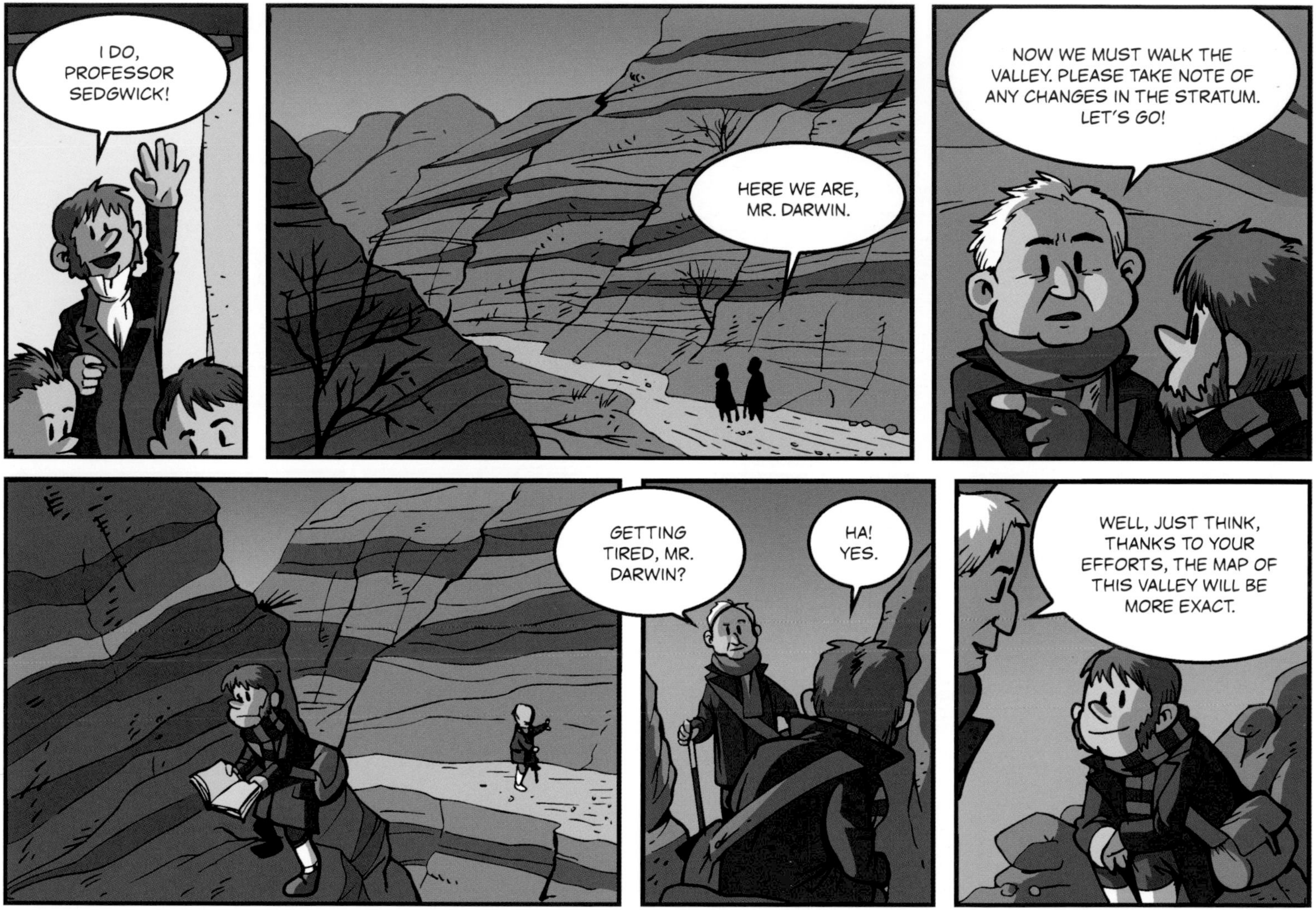
I DO, PROFESSOR SEDGWICK!
HERE WE ARE, MR. DARWIN.
NOW WE MUST WALK THE VALLEY. PLEASE TAKE NOTE OF ANY CHANGES IN THE STRATUM. LET'S GO!
GETTING TIRED, MR. DARWIN?
HA! YES.
WELL, JUST THINK, THANKS TO YOUR EFFORTS, THE MAP OF THIS VALLEY WILL BE MORE EXACT.

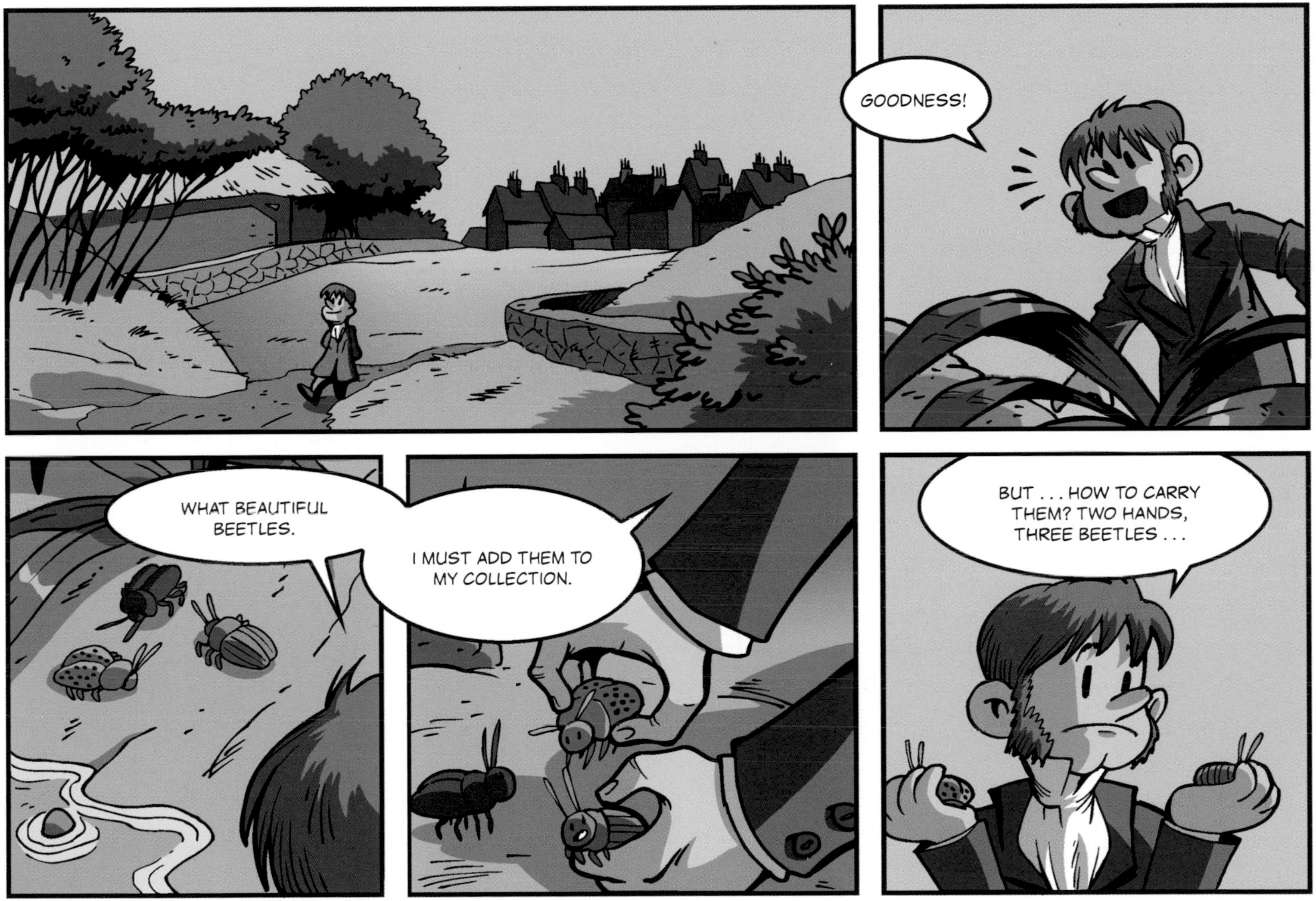
GOODNESS!
WHAT BEAUTIFUL BEETLES.
I MUST ADD THEM TO MY COLLECTION.
BUT . . . HOW TO CARRY THEM? TWO HANDS, THREE BEETLES . . .

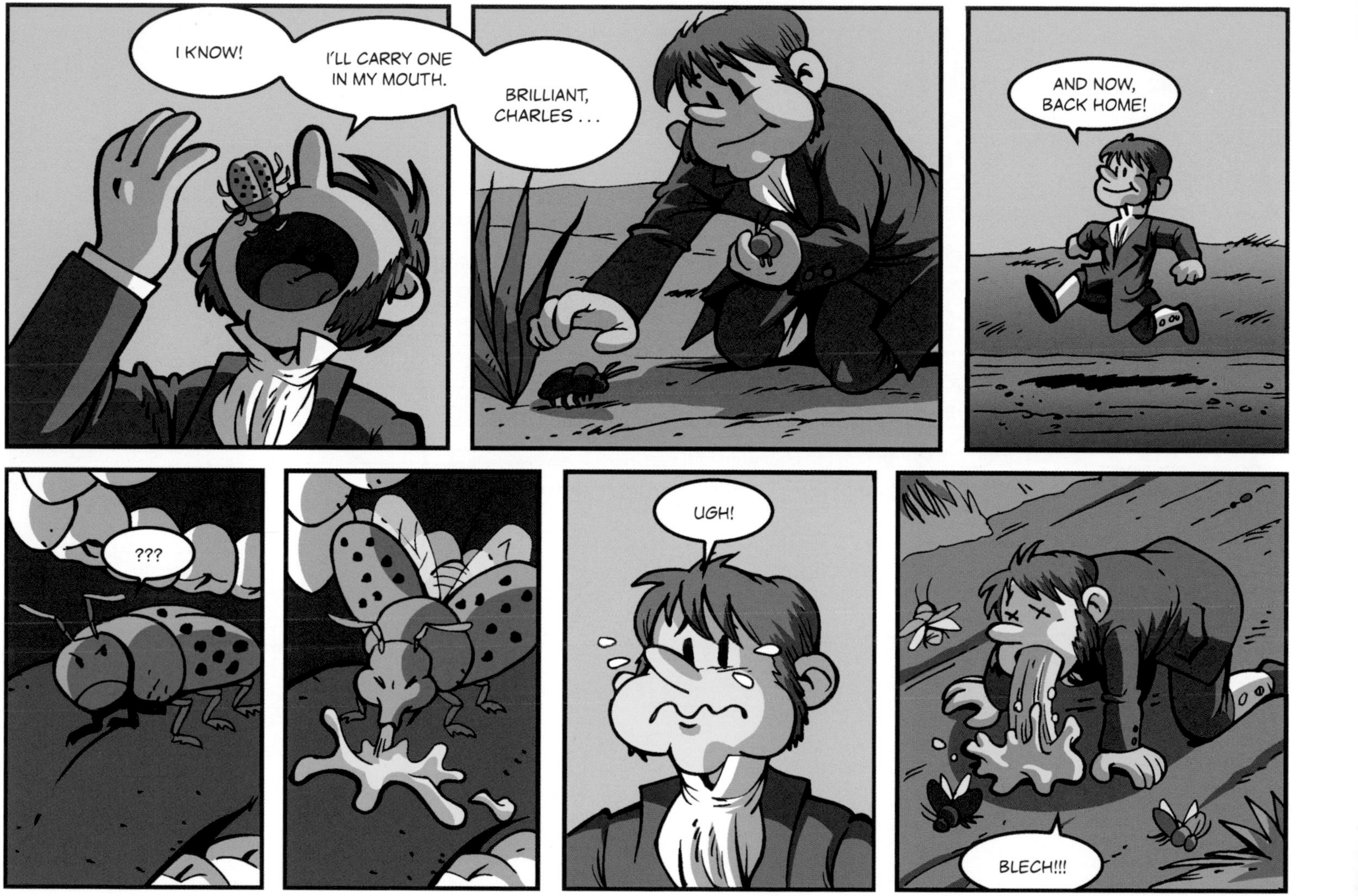
I KNOW!
I'LL CARRY ONE IN MY MOUTH.
BRILLIANT, CHARLES . . .
AND NOW, BACK HOME!
???
UGH!
BLECH!!!

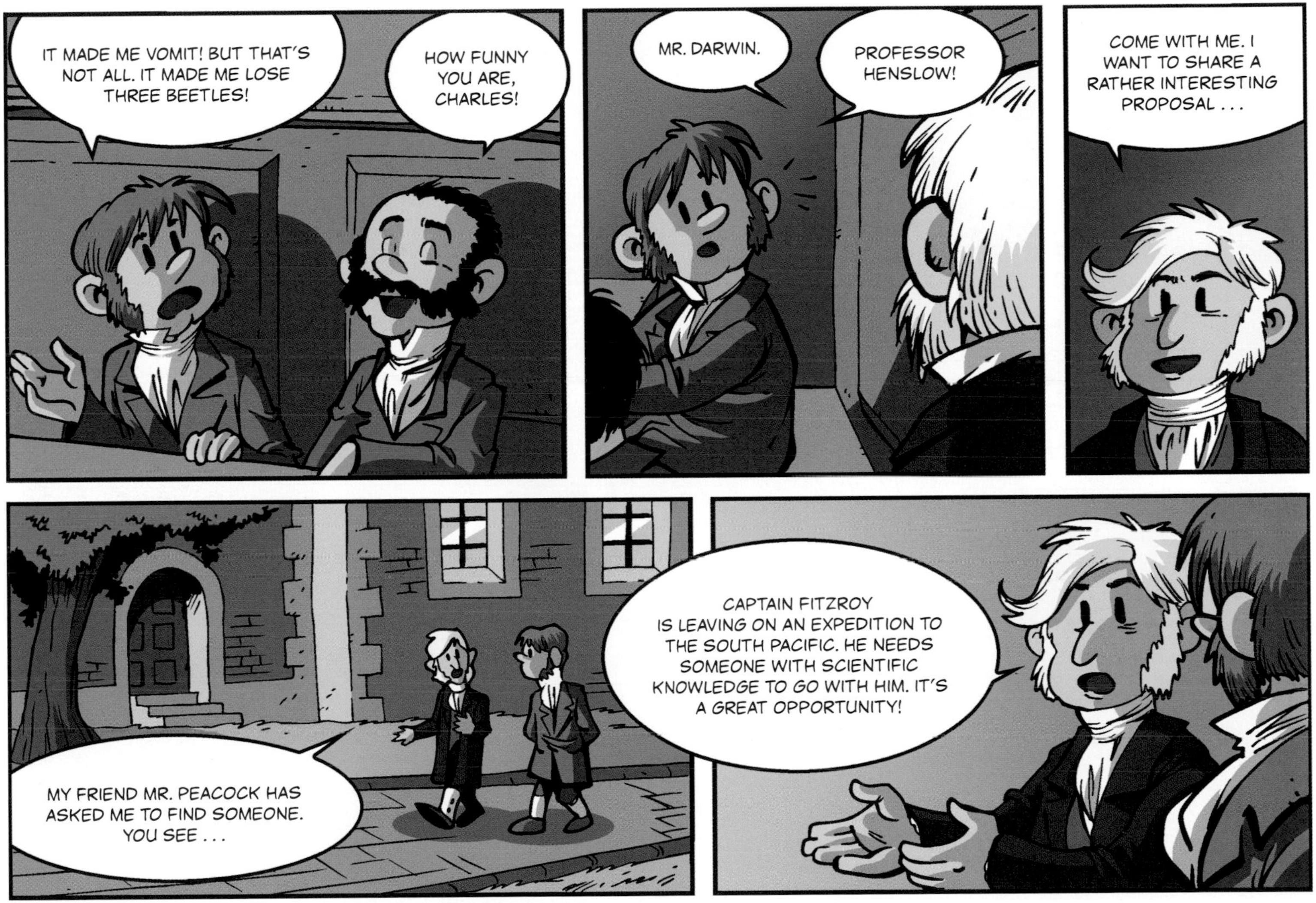
IT MADE ME VOMIT! BUT THAT'S NOT ALL. IT MADE ME LOSE THREE BEETLES!
HOW FUNNY YOU ARE, CHARLES!
MR. DARWIN.
PROFESSOR HENSLOW!
COME WITH ME. I WANT TO SHARE A RATHER INTERESTING PROPOSAL . . .
MY FRIEND MR. PEACOCK HAS ASKED ME TO FIND SOMEONE. YOU SEE . . .
CAPTAIN FITZROY IS LEAVING ON AN EXPEDITION TO THE SOUTH PACIFIC. HE NEEDS SOMEONE WITH SCIENTIFIC KNOWLEDGE TO GO WITH HIM. IT'S A GREAT OPPORTUNITY!

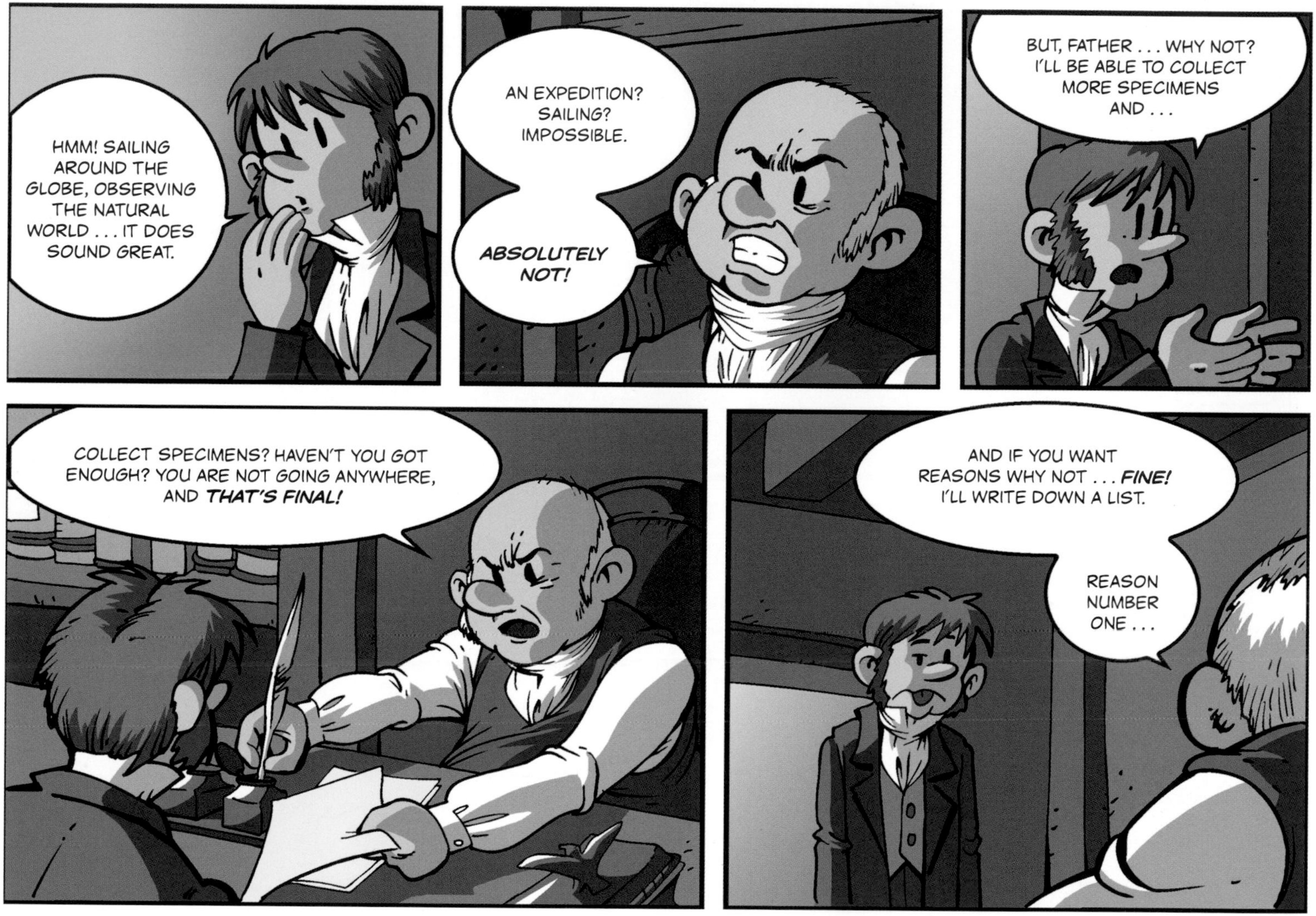
HMM! SAILING AROUND THE GLOBE, OBSERVING THE NATURAL WORLD . . . IT DOES SOUND GREAT.
AN EXPEDITION? SAILING? IMPOSSIBLE.
ABSOLUTELY NOT!
BUT, FATHER . . . WHY NOT? I'LL BE ABLE TO COLLECT MORE SPECIMENS AND . . .
COLLECT SPECIMENS? HAVEN'T YOU GOT ENOUGH? YOU ARE NOT GOING ANYWHERE, AND *THAT'S FINAL!*
AND IF YOU WANT REASONS WHY NOT . . . *FINE!* I'LL WRITE DOWN A LIST.
REASON NUMBER ONE . . .

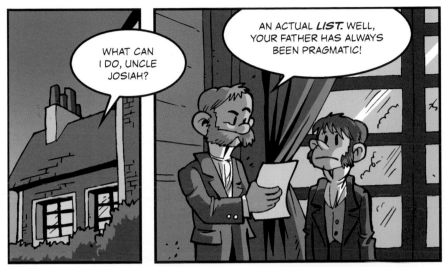

WHAT CAN I DO, UNCLE JOSIAH?

AN ACTUAL *LIST*. WELL, YOUR FATHER HAS ALWAYS BEEN PRAGMATIC!

AND HE DOESN'T SEE THE VALUE IN THE WORK OF A NATURALIST. CLEARLY, HE DOESN'T KNOW HOW IMPORTANT THE STUDY OF NATURE IS . . .

BUT NO MATTER!

IF HE WANTS LISTS, I'LL MAKE ONE RIGHT NOW. LET'S REFUTE HIS ARGUMENTS . . .

WHAT'S THIS? FROM MY BROTHER-IN-LAW?

HAVE COURAGE, CHARLES. NOW THAT HE'S READ OUR ARGUMENTS, WE'LL CONVINCE HIM . . .

I KNOW WHY YOU'VE COME, BUT WE DON'T NEED TO SPEAK ANOTHER WORD ABOUT IT. YOUR LIST HAS CONVINCED ME. CHARLES, YOU MAY *GO* ON THAT VOYAGE!

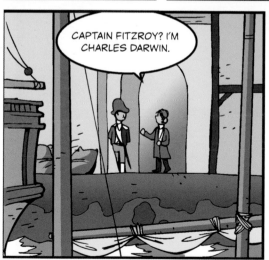

CAPTAIN FITZROY? I'M CHARLES DARWIN.

AH! PEACOCK SENT YOU, DIDN'T HE? WELCOME.

WHEN DO WE LEAVE?

IN FOUR WEEKS.

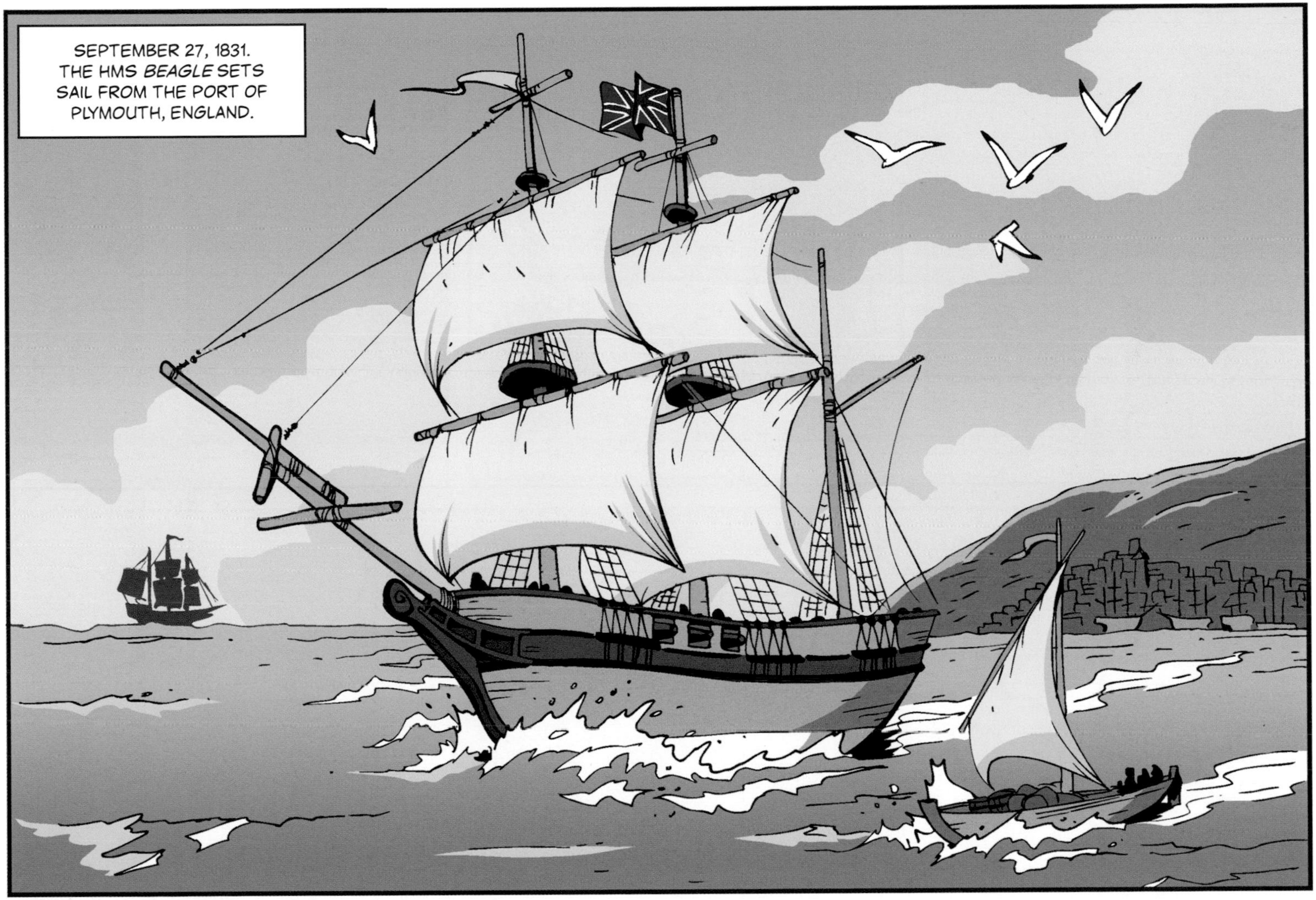
SEPTEMBER 27, 1831. THE HMS *BEAGLE* SETS SAIL FROM THE PORT OF PLYMOUTH, ENGLAND.

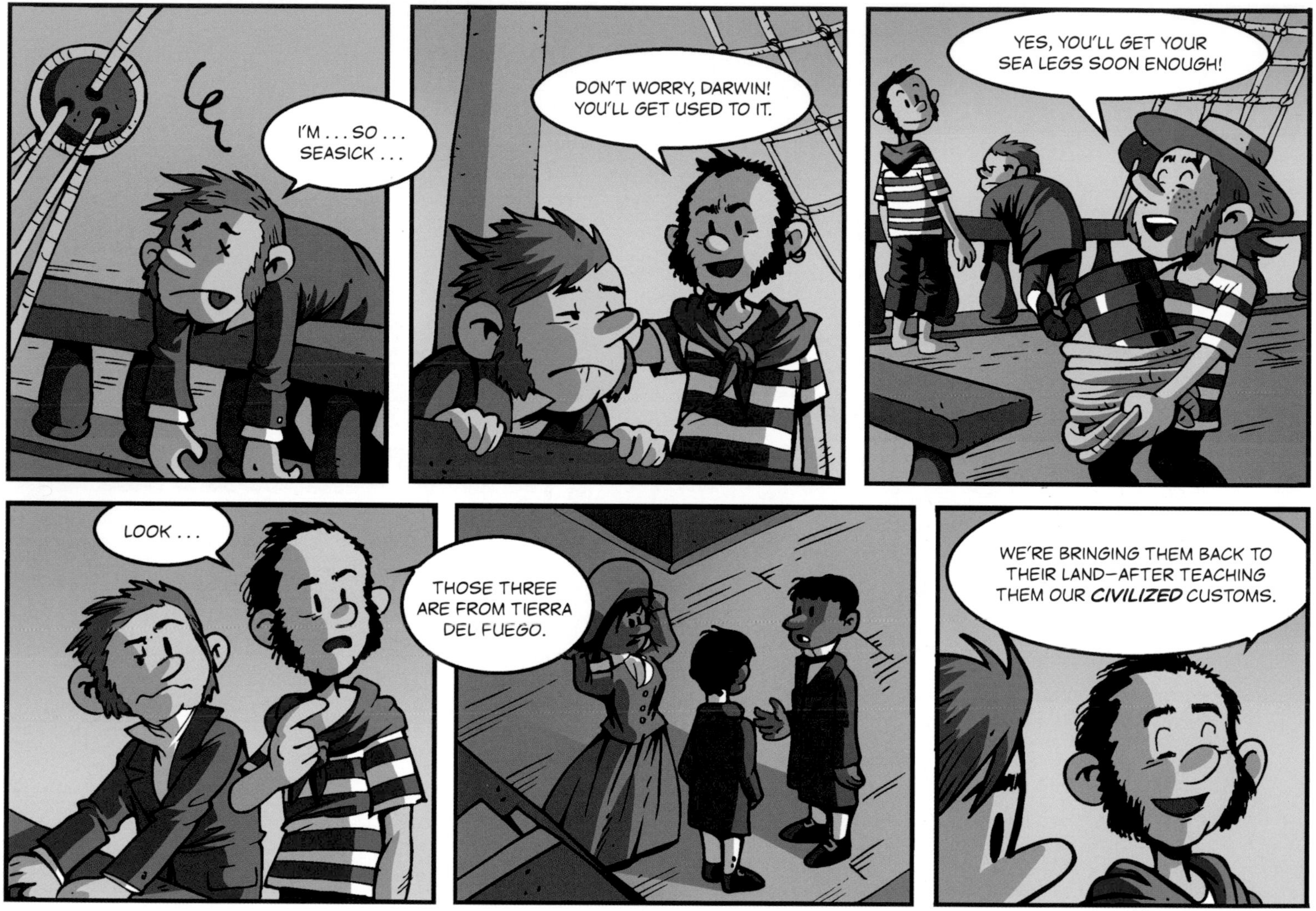
I'M . . . SO . . . SEASICK . . .
DON'T WORRY, DARWIN! YOU'LL GET USED TO IT.
YES, YOU'LL GET YOUR SEA LEGS SOON ENOUGH!
LOOK . . .
THOSE THREE ARE FROM TIERRA DEL FUEGO.
WE'RE BRINGING THEM BACK TO THEIR LAND—AFTER TEACHING THEM OUR *CIVILIZED* CUSTOMS.

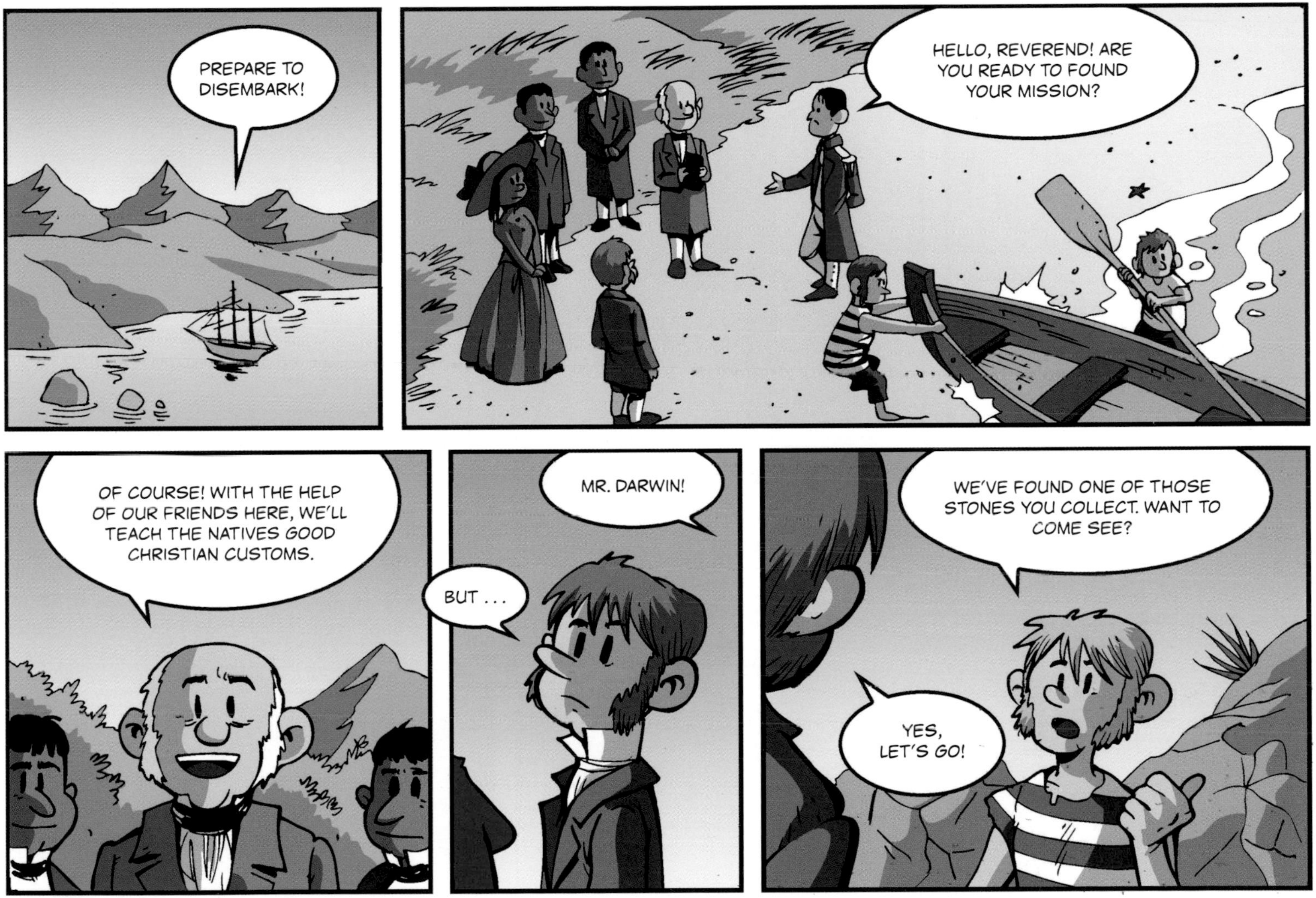
PREPARE TO DISEMBARK!
HELLO, REVEREND! ARE YOU READY TO FOUND YOUR MISSION?
OF COURSE! WITH THE HELP OF OUR FRIENDS HERE, WE'LL TEACH THE NATIVES GOOD CHRISTIAN CUSTOMS.
MR. DARWIN!
BUT . . .
WE'VE FOUND ONE OF THOSE STONES YOU COLLECT. WANT TO COME SEE?
YES, LET'S GO!

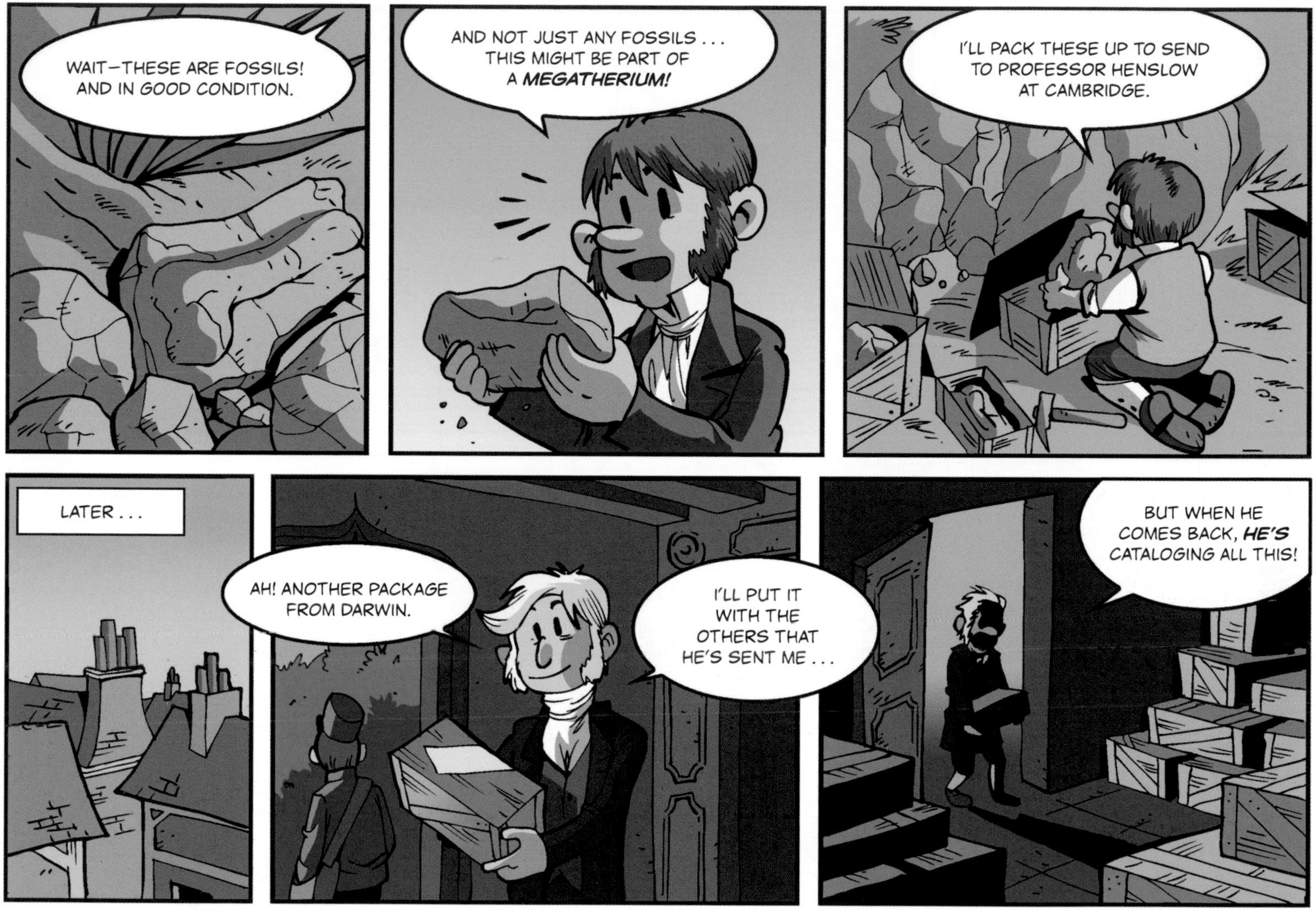
WAIT—THESE ARE FOSSILS! AND IN GOOD CONDITION.
AND NOT JUST ANY FOSSILS . . . THIS MIGHT BE PART OF A **MEGATHERIUM!**
I'LL PACK THESE UP TO SEND TO PROFESSOR HENSLOW AT CAMBRIDGE.
LATER . . .
AH! ANOTHER PACKAGE FROM DARWIN.
I'LL PUT IT WITH THE OTHERS THAT HE'S SENT ME . . .
BUT WHEN HE COMES BACK, **HE'S** CATALOGING ALL THIS!

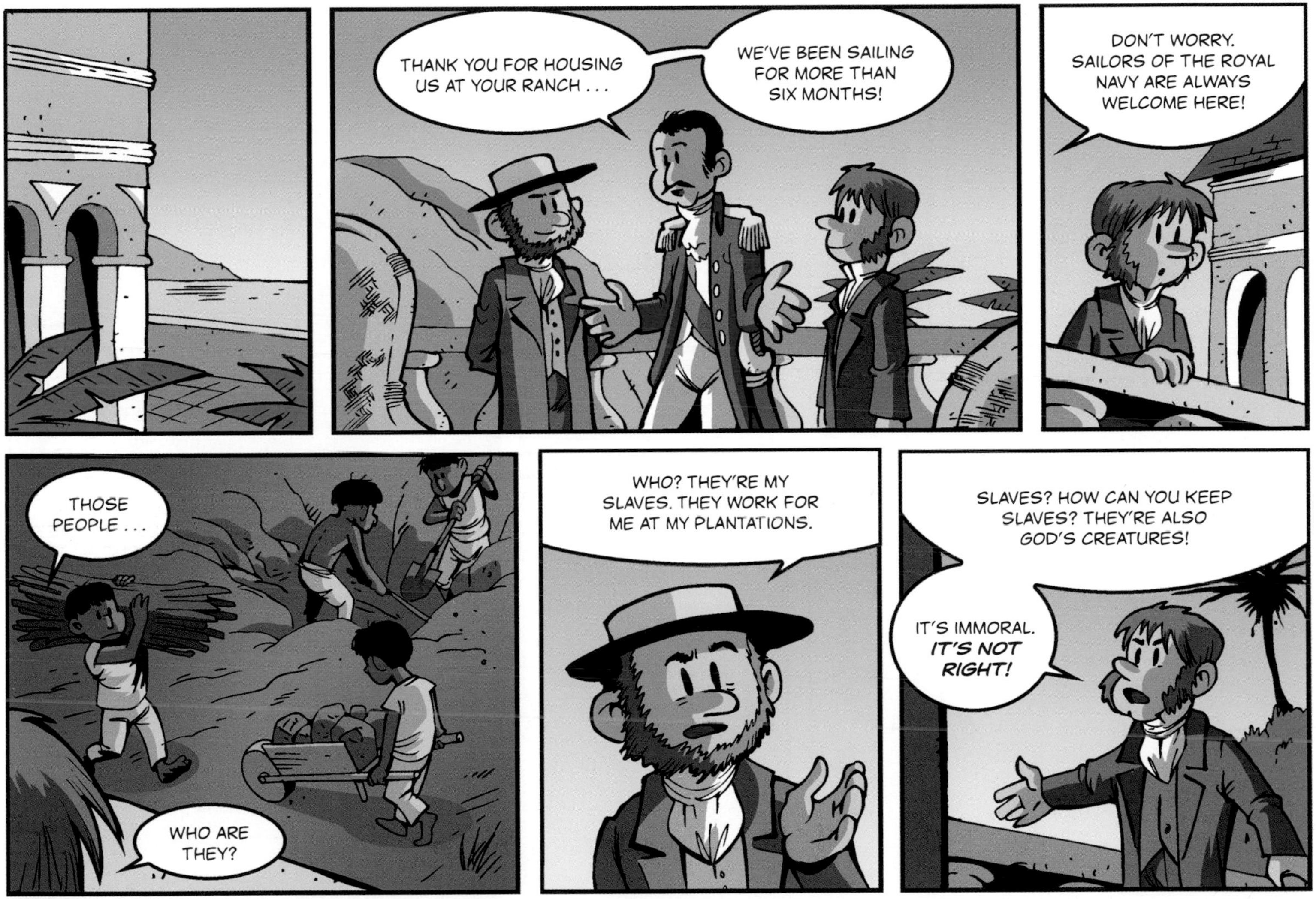
THANK YOU FOR HOUSING US AT YOUR RANCH . . .
WE'VE BEEN SAILING FOR MORE THAN SIX MONTHS!
DON'T WORRY. SAILORS OF THE ROYAL NAVY ARE ALWAYS WELCOME HERE!
THOSE PEOPLE . . .
WHO ARE THEY?
WHO? THEY'RE MY SLAVES. THEY WORK FOR ME AT MY PLANTATIONS.
SLAVES? HOW CAN YOU KEEP SLAVES? THEY'RE ALSO GOD'S CREATURES!
IT'S IMMORAL. ***IT'S NOT RIGHT!***

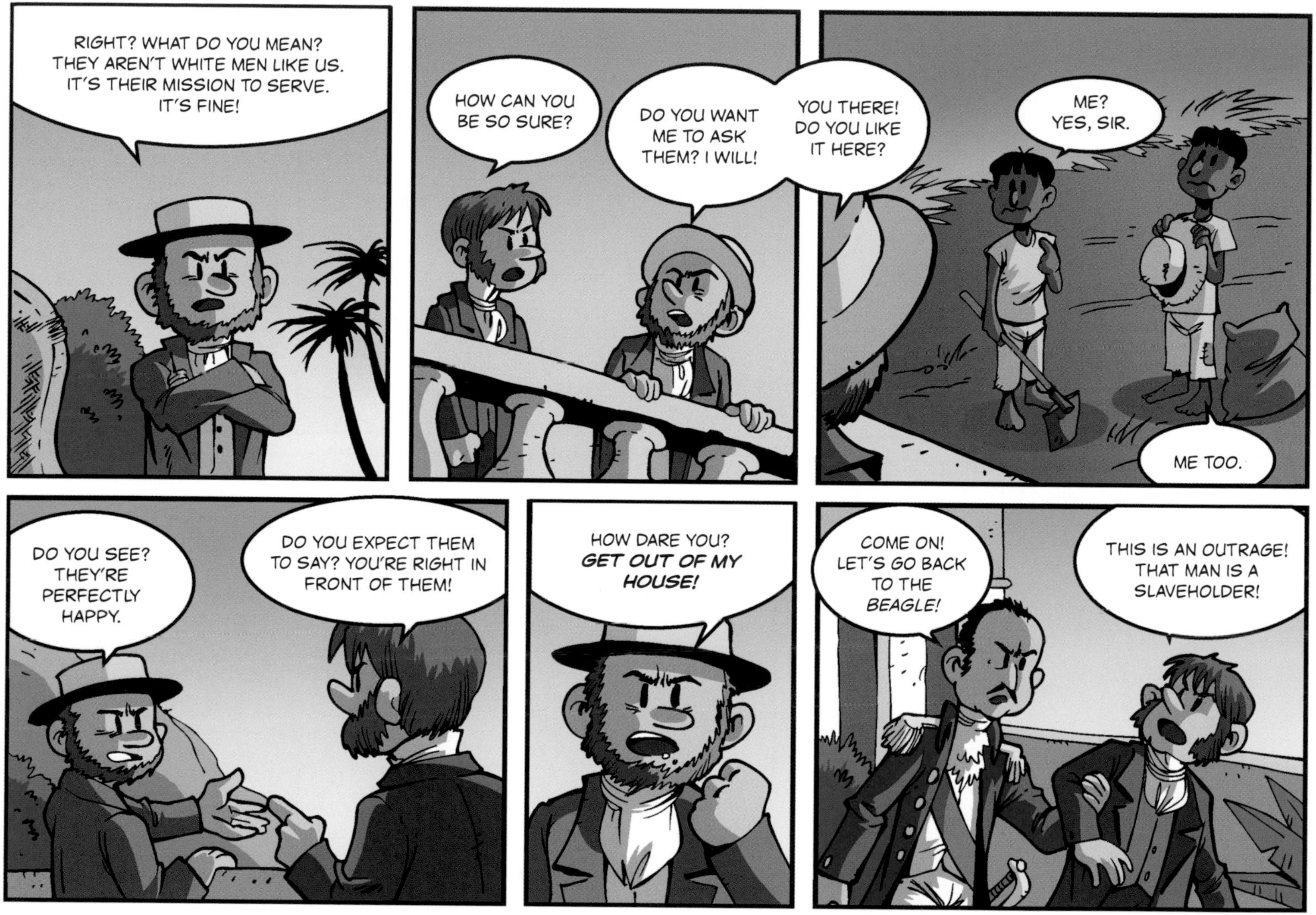
RIGHT? WHAT DO YOU MEAN? THEY AREN'T WHITE MEN LIKE US. IT'S THEIR MISSION TO SERVE. IT'S FINE!
HOW CAN YOU BE SO SURE?
DO YOU WANT ME TO ASK THEM? I WILL!
YOU THERE! DO YOU LIKE IT HERE?
ME? YES, SIR.
ME TOO.
DO YOU SEE? THEY'RE PERFECTLY HAPPY.
DO YOU EXPECT THEM TO SAY? YOU'RE RIGHT IN FRONT OF THEM!
HOW DARE YOU? ***GET OUT OF MY HOUSE!***
COME ON! LET'S GO BACK TO THE *BEAGLE!*
THIS IS AN OUTRAGE! THAT MAN IS A SLAVEHOLDER!

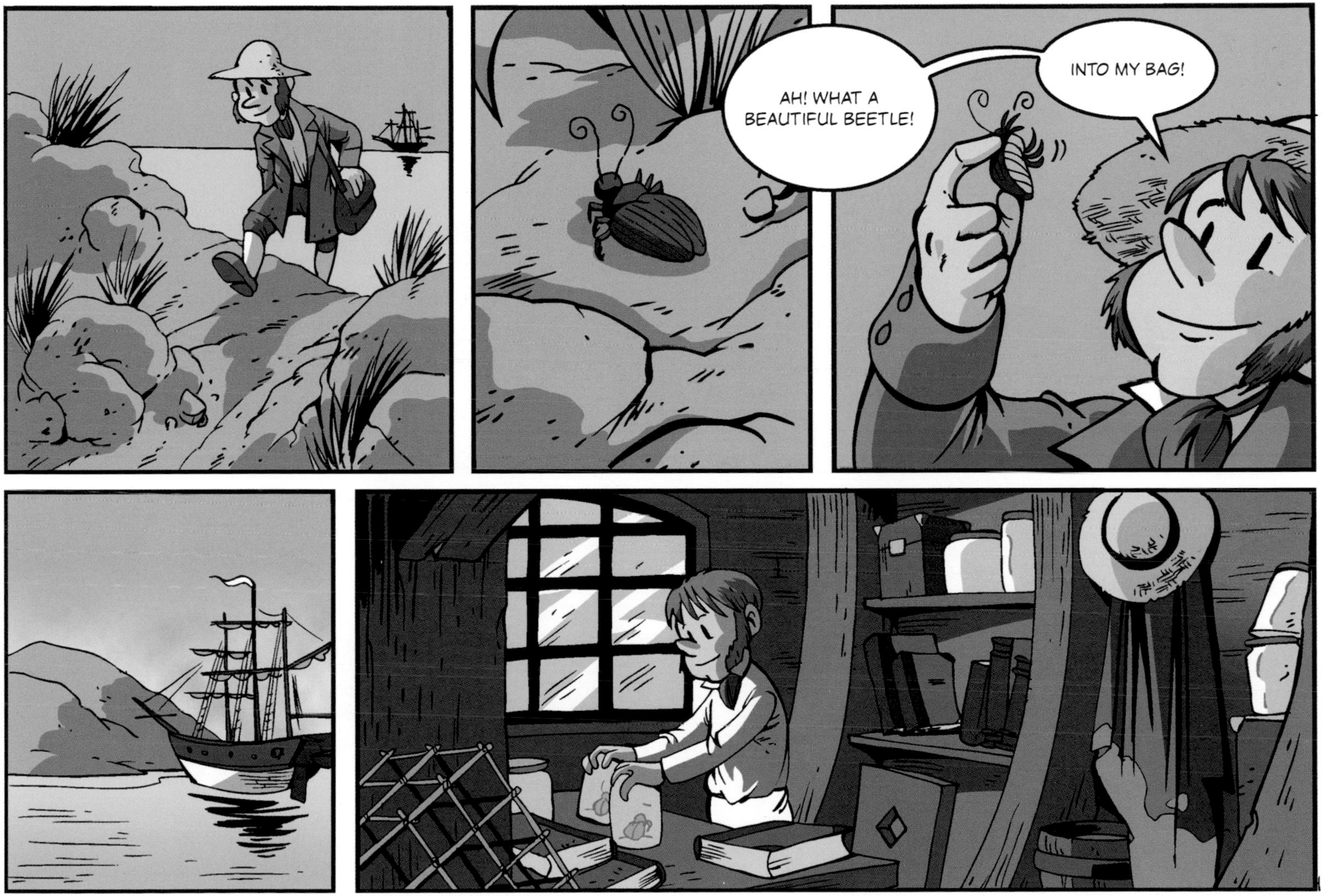
AH! WHAT A BEAUTIFUL BEETLE!
INTO MY BAG!

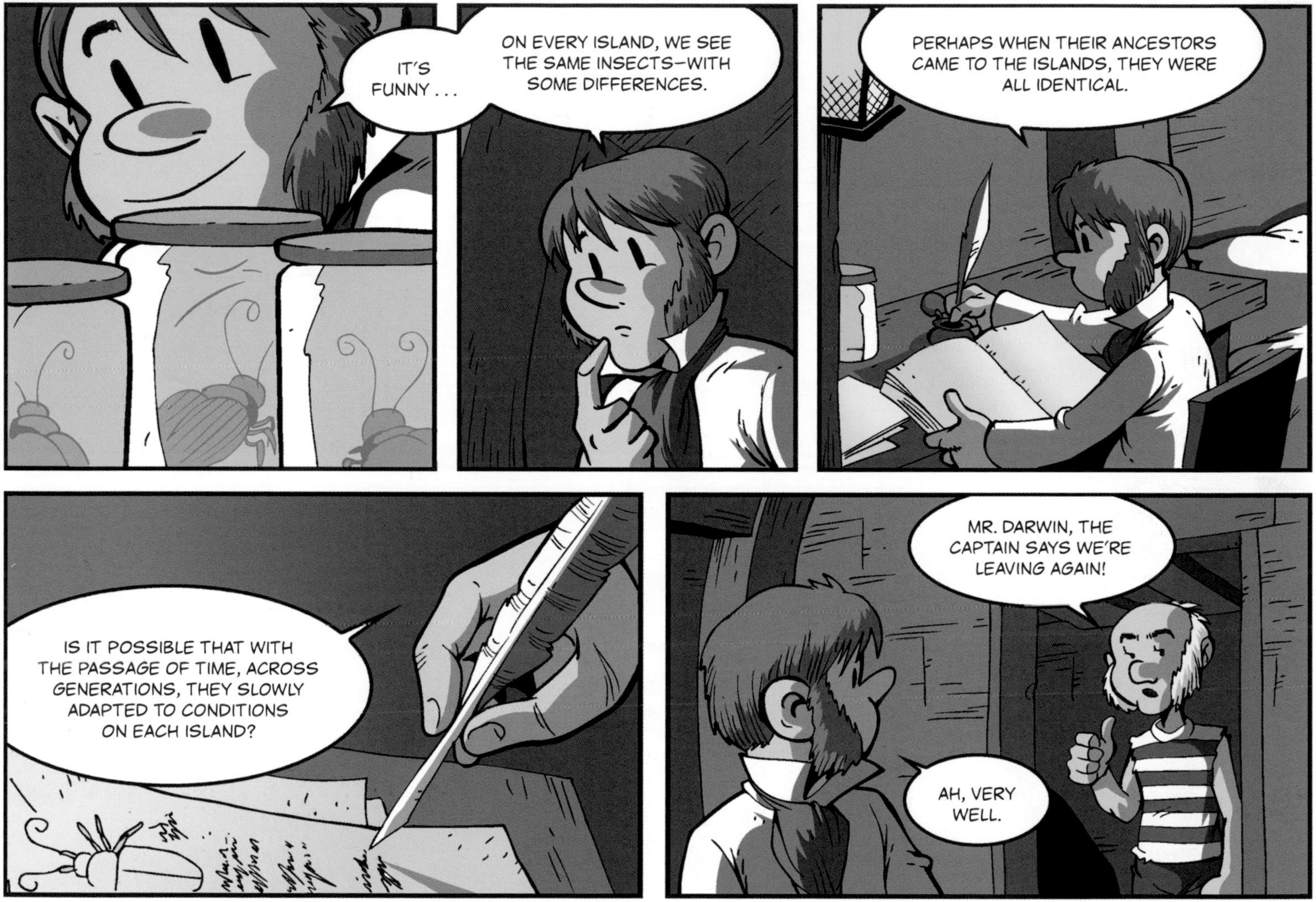
IT'S FUNNY . . .
ON EVERY ISLAND, WE SEE THE SAME INSECTS—WITH SOME DIFFERENCES.
PERHAPS WHEN THEIR ANCESTORS CAME TO THE ISLANDS, THEY WERE ALL IDENTICAL.
IS IT POSSIBLE THAT WITH THE PASSAGE OF TIME, ACROSS GENERATIONS, THEY SLOWLY ADAPTED TO CONDITIONS ON EACH ISLAND?
MR. DARWIN, THE CAPTAIN SAYS WE'RE LEAVING AGAIN!
AH, VERY WELL.

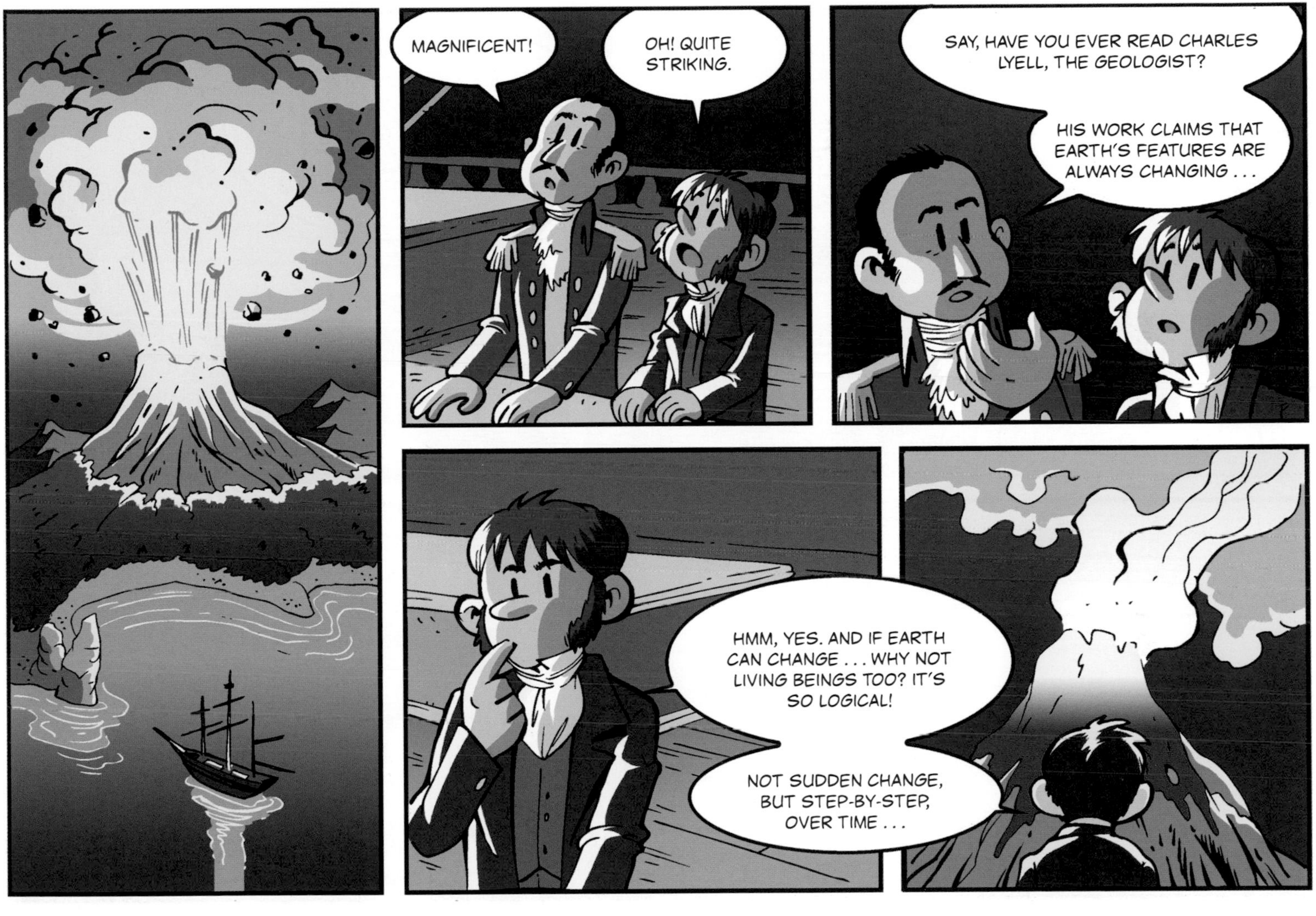
MAGNIFICENT!
OH! QUITE STRIKING.
SAY, HAVE YOU EVER READ CHARLES LYELL, THE GEOLOGIST?
HIS WORK CLAIMS THAT EARTH'S FEATURES ARE ALWAYS CHANGING . . .
HMM, YES. AND IF EARTH CAN CHANGE . . . WHY NOT LIVING BEINGS TOO? IT'S SO LOGICAL!
NOT SUDDEN CHANGE, BUT STEP-BY-STEP, OVER TIME . . .

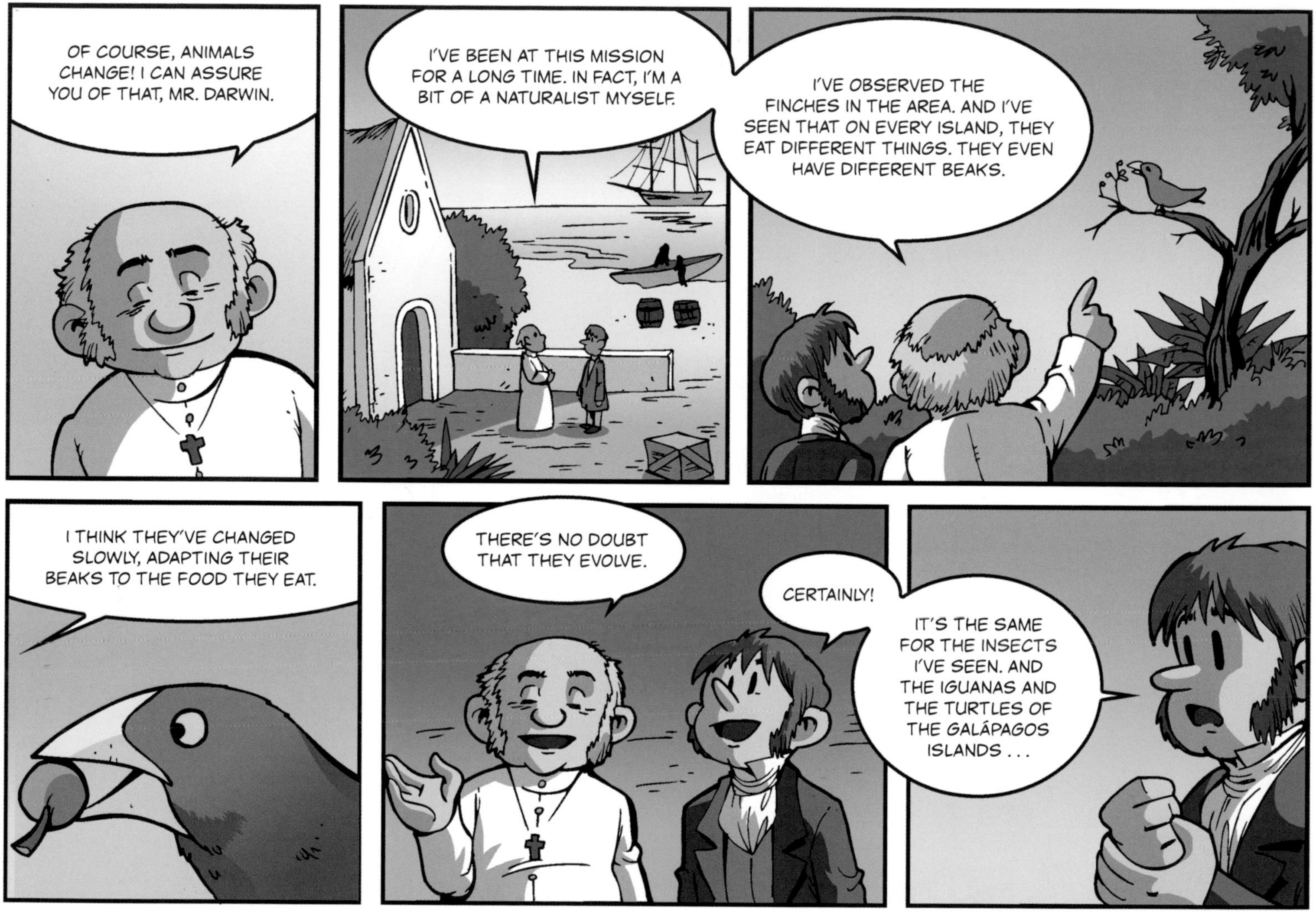
OF COURSE, ANIMALS CHANGE! I CAN ASSURE YOU OF THAT, MR. DARWIN.
I'VE BEEN AT THIS MISSION FOR A LONG TIME. IN FACT, I'M A BIT OF A NATURALIST MYSELF.
I'VE OBSERVED THE FINCHES IN THE AREA. AND I'VE SEEN THAT ON EVERY ISLAND, THEY EAT DIFFERENT THINGS. THEY EVEN HAVE DIFFERENT BEAKS.
I THINK THEY'VE CHANGED SLOWLY, ADAPTING THEIR BEAKS TO THE FOOD THEY EAT.
THERE'S NO DOUBT THAT THEY EVOLVE.
CERTAINLY!
IT'S THE SAME FOR THE INSECTS I'VE SEEN. AND THE IGUANAS AND THE TURTLES OF THE GALÁPAGOS ISLANDS . . .

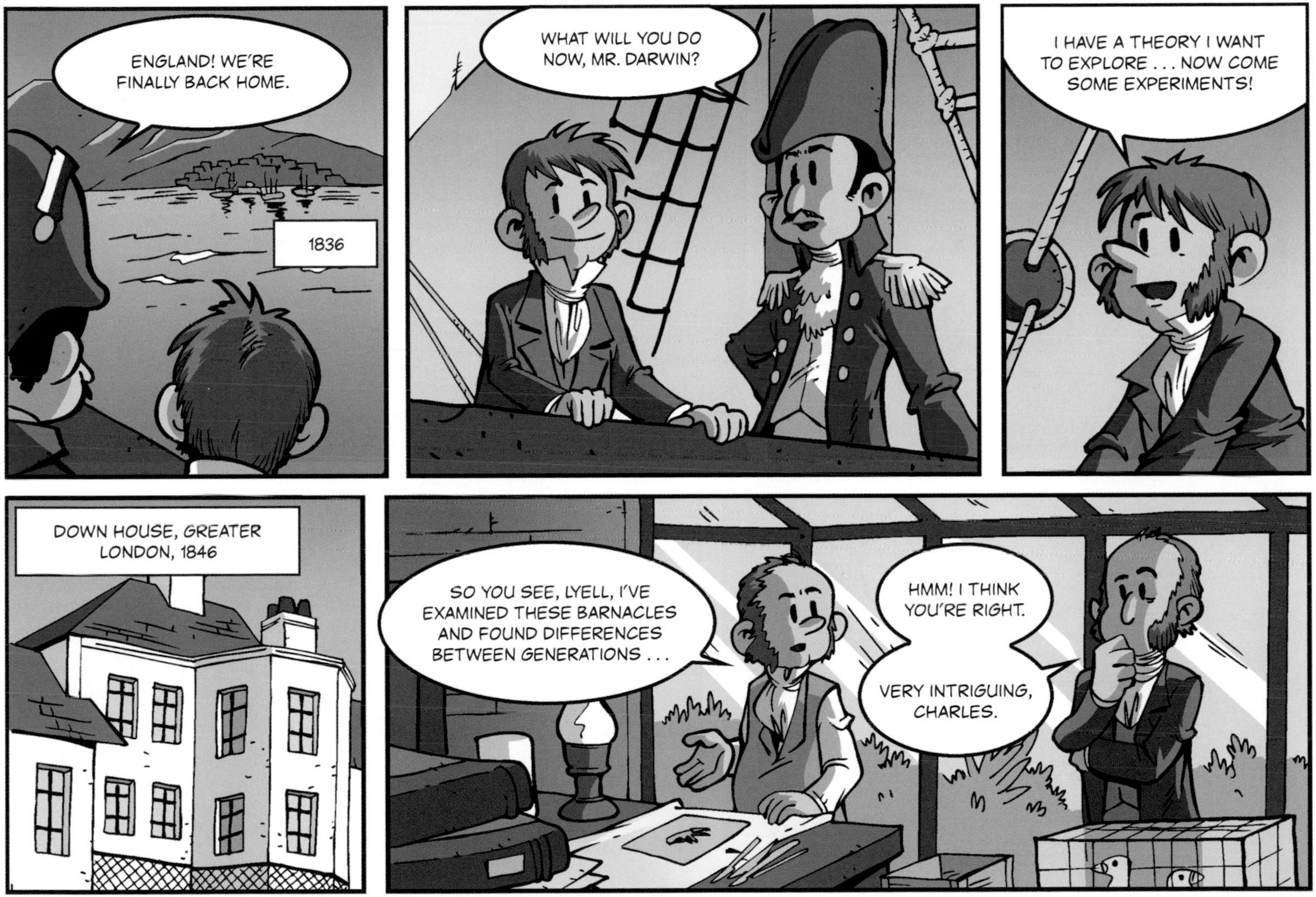
ENGLAND! WE'RE FINALLY BACK HOME.
1836
WHAT WILL YOU DO NOW, MR. DARWIN?
I HAVE A THEORY I WANT TO EXPLORE . . . NOW COME SOME EXPERIMENTS!
DOWN HOUSE, GREATER LONDON, 1846
SO YOU SEE, LYELL, I'VE EXAMINED THESE BARNACLES AND FOUND DIFFERENCES BETWEEN GENERATIONS . . .
HMM! I THINK YOU'RE RIGHT.
VERY INTRIGUING, CHARLES.

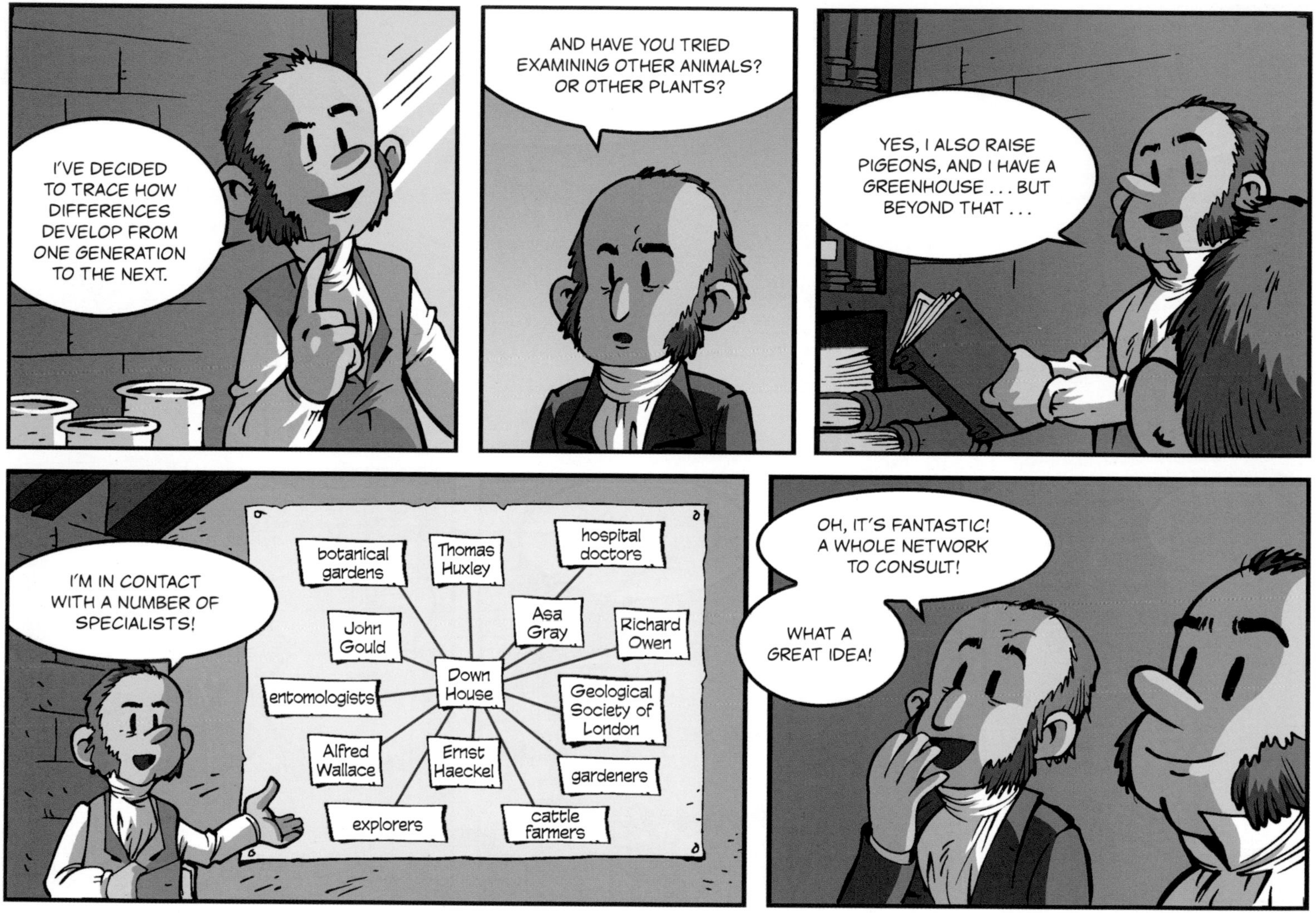
I'VE DECIDED TO TRACE HOW DIFFERENCES DEVELOP FROM ONE GENERATION TO THE NEXT.
AND HAVE YOU TRIED EXAMINING OTHER ANIMALS? OR OTHER PLANTS?
YES, I ALSO RAISE PIGEONS, AND I HAVE A GREENHOUSE . . . BUT BEYOND THAT . . .
I'M IN CONTACT WITH A NUMBER OF SPECIALISTS!
botanical gardens
Thomas Huxley
hospital doctors
John Gould
Asa Gray
Richard Owen
Down House
entomologists
Geological Society of London
Alfred Wallace
Ernst Haeckel
gardeners
explorers
cattle farmers
OH, IT'S FANTASTIC! A WHOLE NETWORK TO CONSULT!
WHAT A GREAT IDEA!

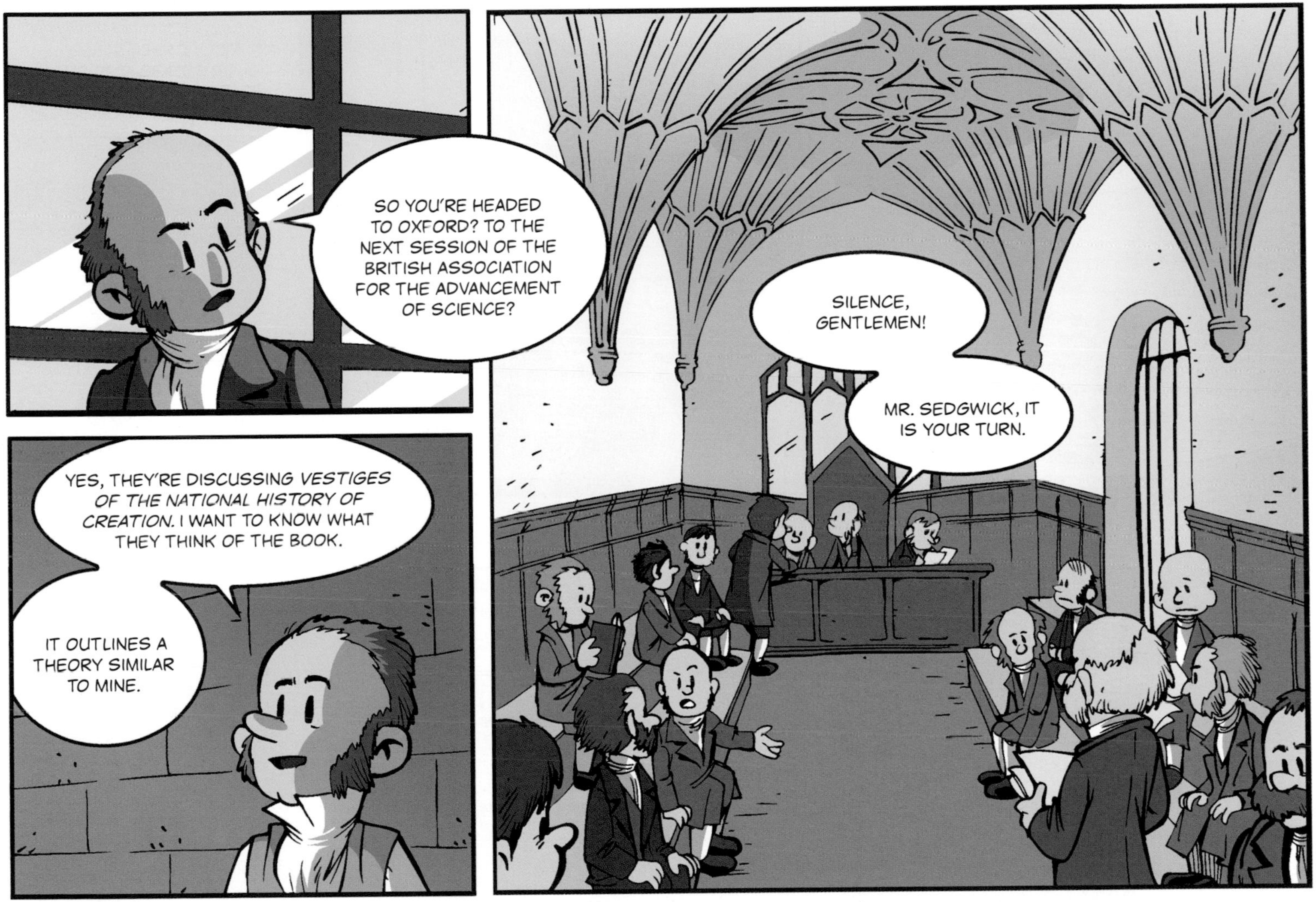
SO YOU'RE HEADED TO OXFORD? TO THE NEXT SESSION OF THE BRITISH ASSOCIATION FOR THE ADVANCEMENT OF SCIENCE?
YES, THEY'RE DISCUSSING *VESTIGES OF THE NATIONAL HISTORY OF CREATION*. I WANT TO KNOW WHAT THEY THINK OF THE BOOK.
IT OUTLINES A THEORY SIMILAR TO MINE.
SILENCE, GENTLEMEN!
MR. SEDGWICK, IT IS YOUR TURN.

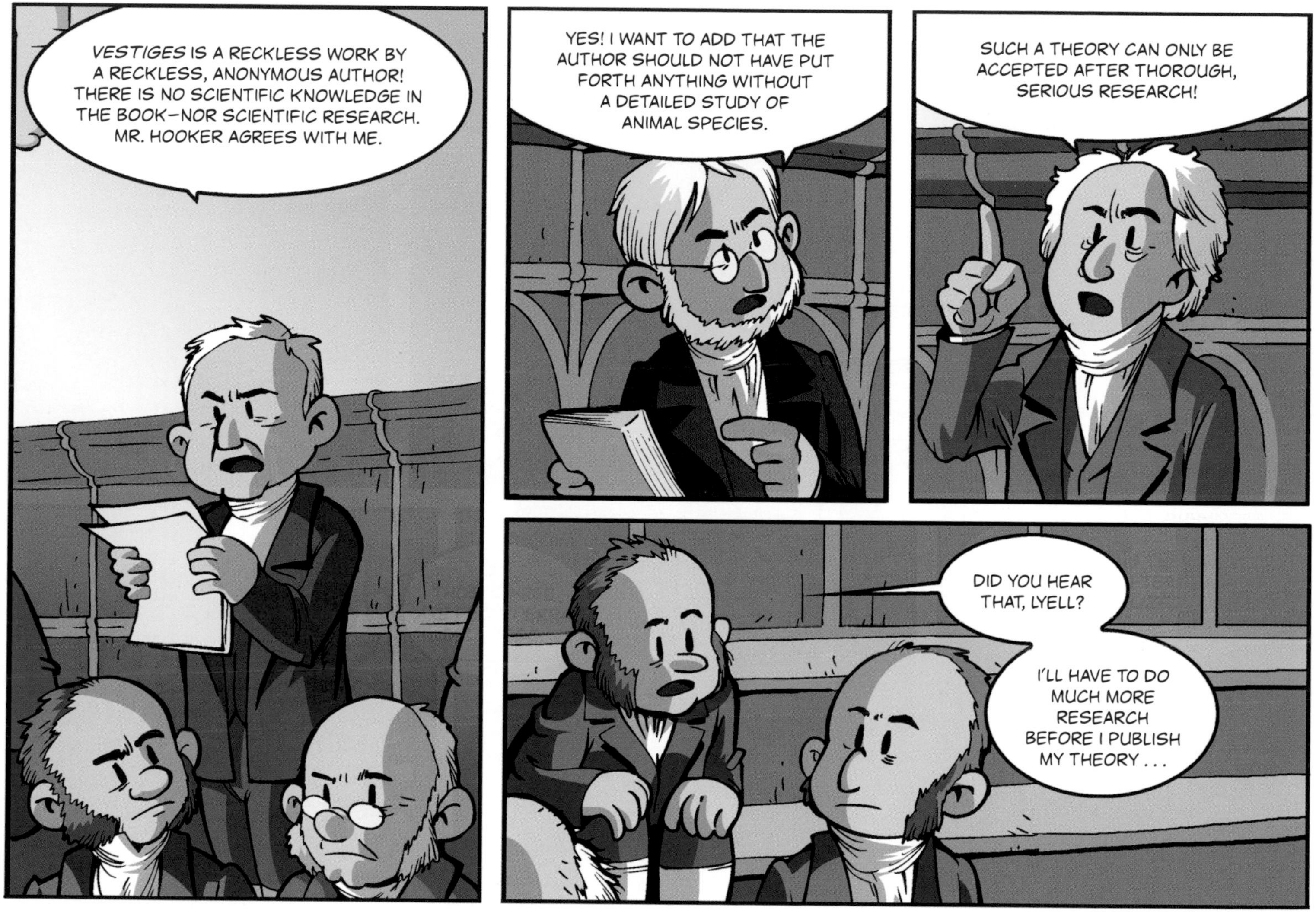
VESTIGES IS A RECKLESS WORK BY A RECKLESS, ANONYMOUS AUTHOR! THERE IS NO SCIENTIFIC KNOWLEDGE IN THE BOOK—NOR SCIENTIFIC RESEARCH. MR. HOOKER AGREES WITH ME.
YES! I WANT TO ADD THAT THE AUTHOR SHOULD NOT HAVE PUT FORTH ANYTHING WITHOUT A DETAILED STUDY OF ANIMAL SPECIES.
SUCH A THEORY CAN ONLY BE ACCEPTED AFTER THOROUGH, SERIOUS RESEARCH!
DID YOU HEAR THAT, LYELL?
I'LL HAVE TO DO MUCH MORE RESEARCH BEFORE I PUBLISH MY THEORY . . .

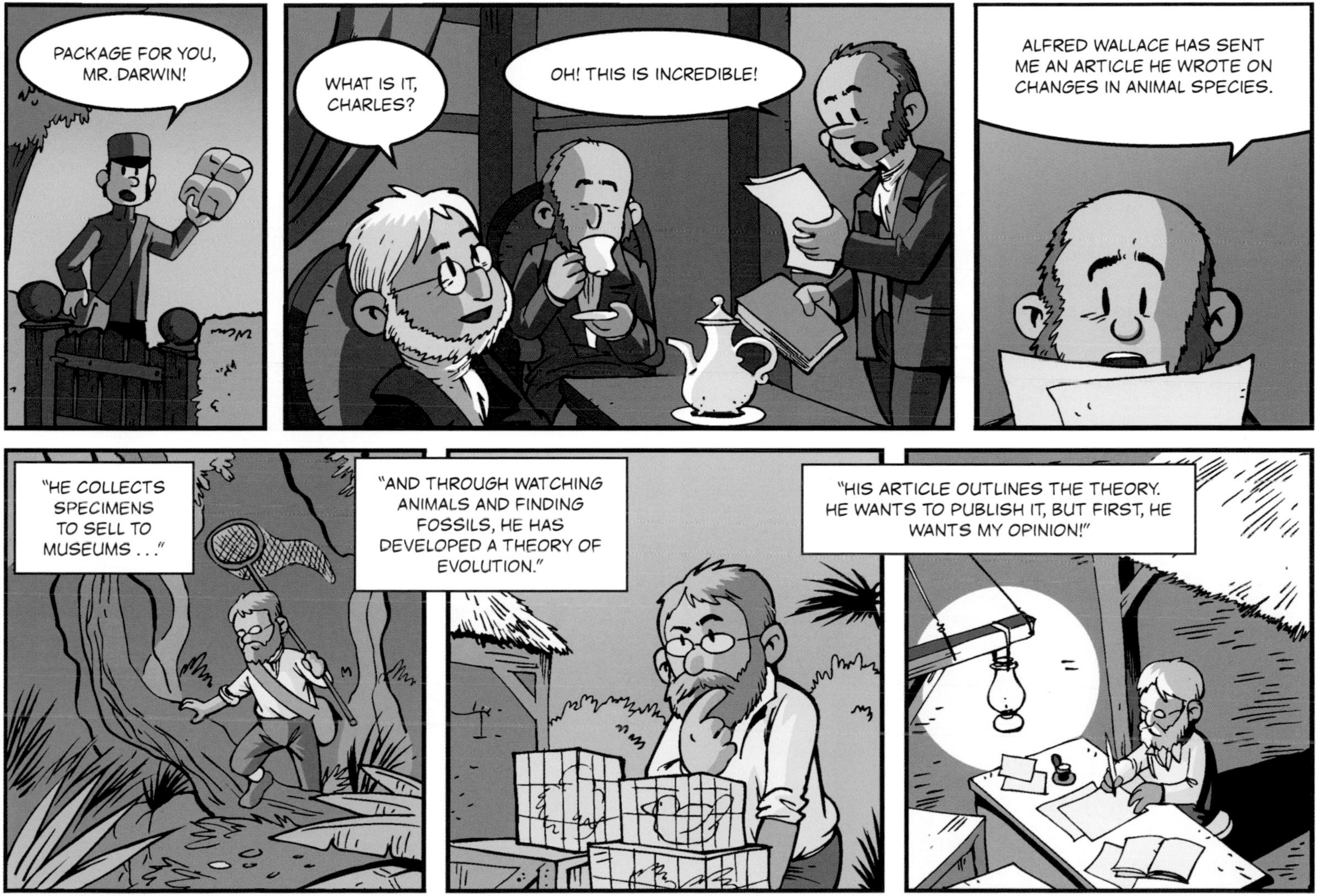
PACKAGE FOR YOU, MR. DARWIN!
WHAT IS IT, CHARLES?
OH! THIS IS INCREDIBLE!
ALFRED WALLACE HAS SENT ME AN ARTICLE HE WROTE ON CHANGES IN ANIMAL SPECIES.
"HE COLLECTS SPECIMENS TO SELL TO MUSEUMS . . ."
"AND THROUGH WATCHING ANIMALS AND FINDING FOSSILS, HE HAS DEVELOPED A THEORY OF EVOLUTION."
"HIS ARTICLE OUTLINES THE THEORY. HE WANTS TO PUBLISH IT, BUT FIRST, HE WANTS MY OPINION!"

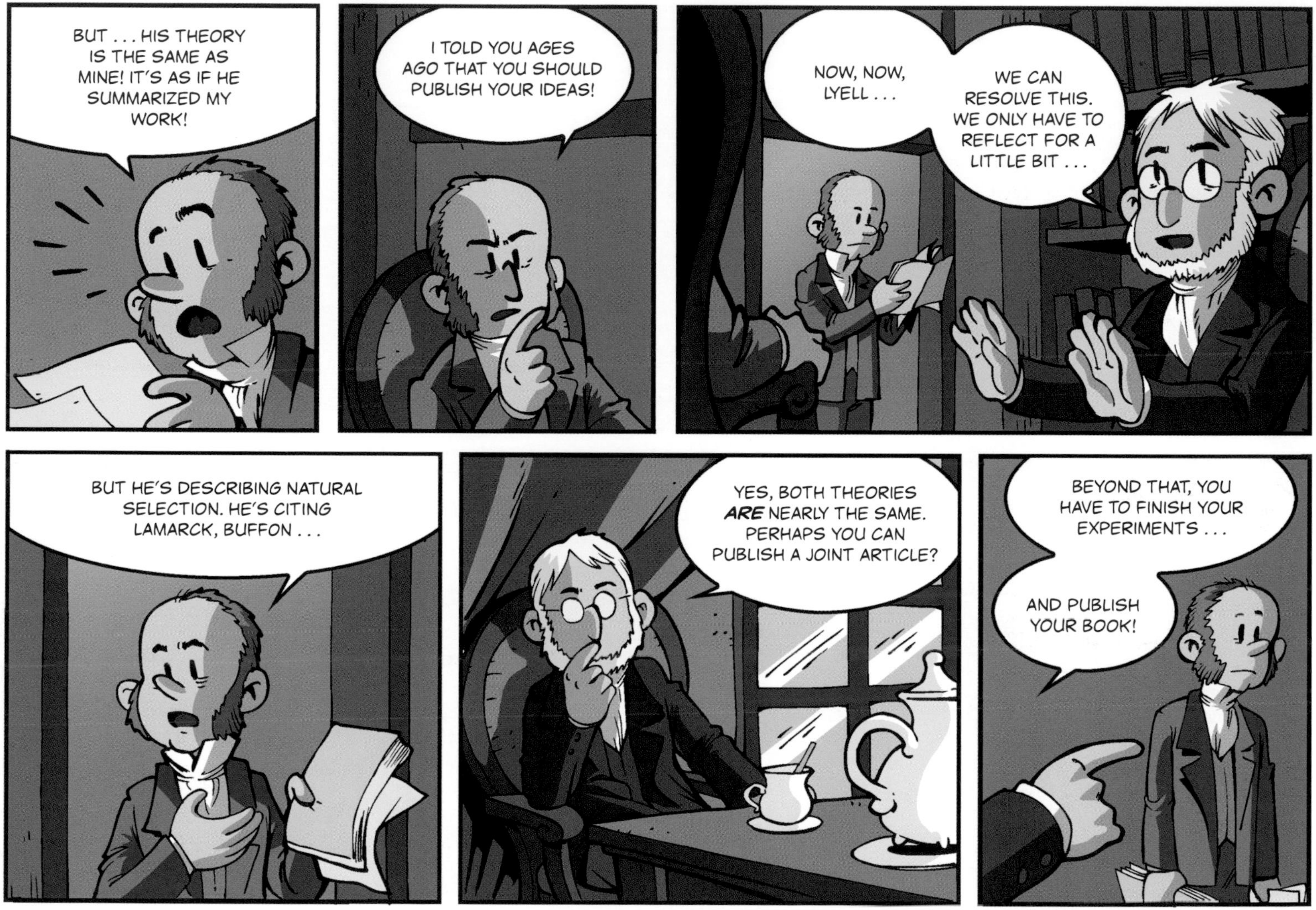
BUT . . . HIS THEORY IS THE SAME AS MINE! IT'S AS IF HE SUMMARIZED MY WORK!
I TOLD YOU AGES AGO THAT YOU SHOULD PUBLISH YOUR IDEAS!
NOW, NOW, LYELL . . .
WE CAN RESOLVE THIS. WE ONLY HAVE TO REFLECT FOR A LITTLE BIT . . .
BUT HE'S DESCRIBING NATURAL SELECTION. HE'S CITING LAMARCK, BUFFON . . .
YES, BOTH THEORIES ***ARE*** NEARLY THE SAME. PERHAPS YOU CAN PUBLISH A JOINT ARTICLE?
BEYOND THAT, YOU HAVE TO FINISH YOUR EXPERIMENTS . . .
AND PUBLISH YOUR BOOK!

I'LL WRITE TO WALLACE AND PROPOSE . . .

"THE JOINT PUBLICATION OF AN ARTICLE WITH MR. DARWIN."

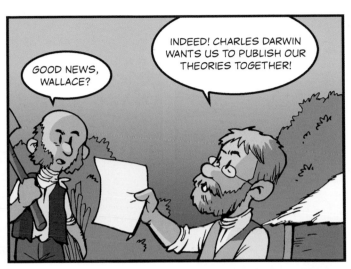

GOOD NEWS, WALLACE?

INDEED! CHARLES DARWIN WANTS US TO PUBLISH OUR THEORIES TOGETHER!

HOW'S YOUR WRITING GOING?

I'M NEARLY FINISHED! REMEMBER, THIS COVERS MANY YEARS OF RESEARCH.

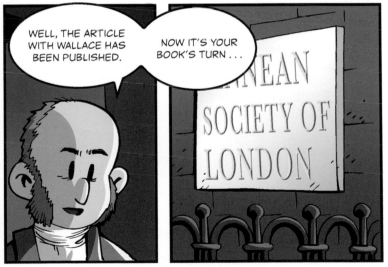

WELL, THE ARTICLE WITH WALLACE HAS BEEN PUBLISHED.

NOW IT'S YOUR BOOK'S TURN . . .

NEAN SOCIETY OF LONDON

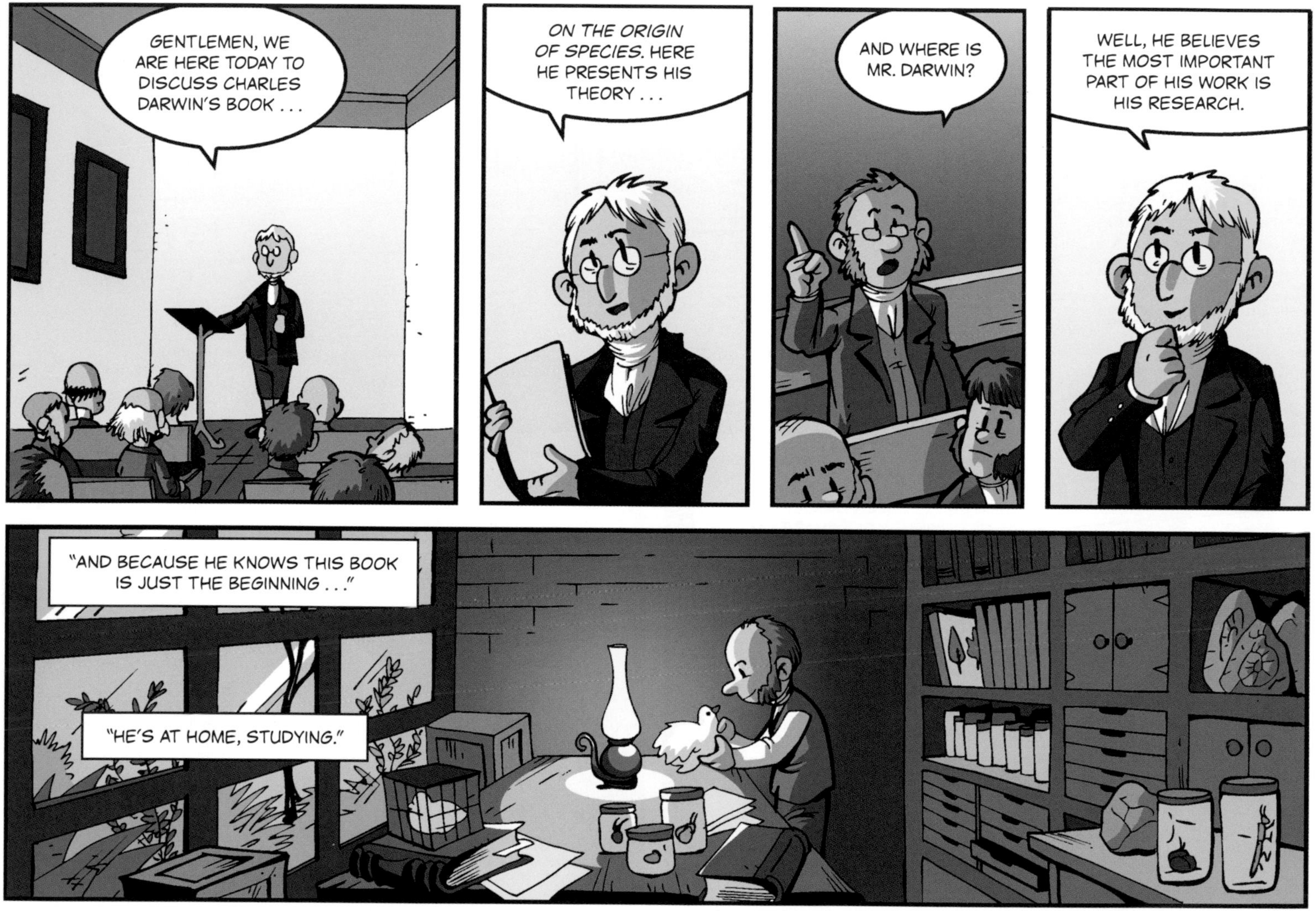
GENTLEMEN, WE ARE HERE TODAY TO DISCUSS CHARLES DARWIN'S BOOK . . .
ON THE ORIGIN OF SPECIES. HERE HE PRESENTS HIS THEORY . . .
AND WHERE IS MR. DARWIN?
WELL, HE BELIEVES THE MOST IMPORTANT PART OF HIS WORK IS HIS RESEARCH.
"AND BECAUSE HE KNOWS THIS BOOK IS JUST THE BEGINNING . . ."
"HE'S AT HOME, STUDYING."

TIMELINE

1809 Charles Darwin is born in Shrewsbury, England, on February 12.

1825 He begins medical school in Edinburgh, England.

1831 He leaves for his expedition on the HMS *Beagle* on September 27.

1836 He returns to England after five years of collecting samples around the world.

1839 He marries Emma Wedgwood on January 29.

1856 He begins writing a book on natural selection on the advice of Charles Lyell.

1859 *On the Origin of Species* is published in London on November 24.

1864 Darwin wins the Copley Medal, an award for scientific achievement from the Royal Society of London.

1871 He publishes *The Descent of Man*, which applies the theory of evolution to human development.

1882 He dies at the age of seventy-three on April 26.

GLOSSARY

ABDOMEN: the region of the body that holds the stomach and other organs

ANATOMY: the scientific study of the structure of humans and animals

CATALOG: to make a list of scientific samples and their properties

DISEMBARK: to leave a ship

DISSECT: to cut apart a dead animal or person for scientific study

EVOLUTION: a living organism's gradual change over time

FINANCIER: someone who helps manage large amounts of money

GALÁPAGOS ISLANDS: an island chain in the Pacific Ocean

MISSION: the base used by a group of people who seek to convert others to their faith

NATURALIST: a scientist who studies plants and animals in nature

PRAGMATIC: practical and concerned with facts and results

SPECIMENS: samples of plants or animals taken by scientists for research

STRATUM: a layer of rock that is different from the other layers around it

TIERRA DEL FUEGO: a chain of islands at the southern tip of South America

VESTIGES OF THE NATURAL HISTORY OF CREATION: an 1844 book by Robert Chambers that combined several new ideas about evolution. Its author was originally unknown to the scientific community.

FURTHER RESOURCES

Bayarri, Jordi. *Isaac Newton and the Force of Gravity*. Minneapolis: Graphic Universe, 2020.

Charles Darwin Online
      http://darwin-online.org.uk

Famous Scientists: Charles Darwin
      https://www.famousscientists.org/charles-darwin

TED-Ed: "Myths and Misconceptions about Evolution"
      https://www.youtube.com/watch?v=mZt1Gn0R22Q

Zuchora-Walske, Christine. *Key Discoveries in Life Science*. Minneapolis: Lerner Publications, 2015.

INDEX

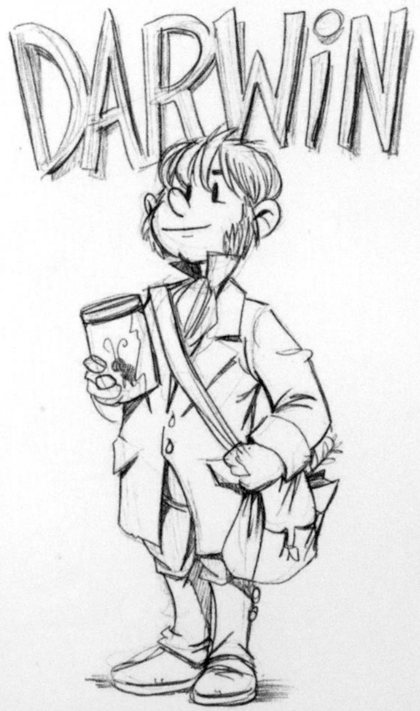
DARWIN